8-1-16 $30.70

ORIGINAL THINKERS™

-TRAILBLAZERS IN-

RELIGION

JEREMY STANGROOM

This edition published in 2015 by:
The Rosen Publishing Group, Inc.
29 East 21st Street
New York, NY 10010

Additional end matter copyright © 2015 by The Rosen
Publishing Group, Inc.

All rights reserved. No part of this book may be
reproduced in any form without permission in writing
from the publisher, except by a reviewer.

Library of Congress Cataloging-in-Publication Date

Stangroom, Jeremy.
Trailblazers in religion/Jeremy Stangroom. — First
Edition.
    pages cm. — (Original thinkers)
Includes bibliographical references and index.
ISBN 978-1-4777-8142-5 (library bound)
1. Religious leaders. I. Title.
BL72.S73 2014
200.92'2—dc23
                                        2014023959

Manufactured in the United States of America

© 2015 ELWIN STREET PRODUCTIONS www.elwinstreet.com

Cover Credits: Statue of Buddha © Leemage/Getty Images; background ©
Roman Sakhno/Shutterstock.com

ORIGINAL THINKERS™

–TRAILBLAZERS IN–
RELIGION

JEREMY STANGROOM

ROSEN
PUBLISHING®

New York

HELIAS HIGH SCHOOL
LIBRARY
Jefferson City, MO

Contents

Introduction

Religion is notoriously difficult to define. The commonsense view, certainly in the West, is that it comprises beliefs and practices that are about, or directed towards, God or gods. This definition works well for the great Abrahamic religions, Judaism, Christianity, and Islam (so called because they trace their lineages back to Abraham, the ancient Semitic patriarch), which account for more than half of the world's religious believers. However, it does not work so well for religions outside the Abrahamic tradition. Buddhism, for example, which is popular in Japan and China, has no clear conception of God, yet it is normally considered a religion. Similarly, the idea of God, or indeed the supernatural at all, is almost entirely absent from Confucianism, the religious philosophy that underpins much of Chinese culture.

Perhaps, then, a better candidate for a definition of religion is that put forward by French sociologist Emile Durkheim (1858–1917). He defined religion as "a unified system of beliefs and practices relative to sacred things." This definition is not perfect — it seems to exclude the highly personal as religious, for example — but it is much closer to the inclusive spirit of this book than the standard God-centered definition of religion.

This book features fifty of the world's most important religious figures. They are prophets, thinkers, theologians, and leaders drawn from the world's great religions, including the three main Abrahamic faiths, Hinduism, Buddhism, Sikhism, and Confucianism. In addition, the book also examines ten concepts — for example, monotheism, deism, and scripture — each of which helps in gaining an understanding of religion that goes beyond the contributions of specific individuals.

The question that always arises in a book of this nature is how it is possible to come up with a specific selection of people. The answer is that there is always something a little arbitrary about who to include and who to leave out. All who are included here have contributed in some significant way to the religious lives of millions of people (even if only by an intellectual ripple-down effect). However, there are clearly other great leaders, theologians, and religious thinkers who could have been included, so there is no claim here that the people in this book are the most important religious figures.

There is an additional issue here that has to do with the relative representation of the various religions in the following pages. Broadly speaking, the larger the religion or religious tradition, the greater the representation. Thus, the Judeo-Christian tradition, which has some 2.2 billion adherents, is represented by twenty-five people, whereas Zoroastrianism, which has at most 2 million devotees, is represented only by its founder, Zarathustra.

The final point to make has to do with religious truth-claims. This book is neutral with respect to the veracity of the claims made by the various religions. These are reported as they exist within their specific traditions, without any attempt external to these traditions to assess the truthfulness or logical consistency of religious beliefs. The point is simply to introduce the great religious figures and their thought.

Dr. Jeremy Stangroom

Jesus of Nazareth

The story of Jesus Christ is better known in the Western world than that of any other person: he was the son of God, born of a virgin, and he lived and died in order to save humanity from their sins. What may be less well known is the detail of his teachings — the message that he wanted to share with humanity as the self-proclaimed "Son of Man."

Born: 6–4 BC, Bethlehem, Israel

Importance: The founder of the Christian religion

Died: Ca. 30 CE, Jerusalem, Israel

The central message of his teaching was that the kingdom of God would soon be ushered in on earth and that people should be prepared for it. In essence, it was a plea for repentance: in order to achieve salvation, it was necessary to meet God's demands, which were embodied in the example of his life.

Jesus suggested that those who wished to be part of the kingdom to come should give up everything in order to return to God, their Father. He did not call for personal loyalty from his followers, just that they live by his example. There is the suggestion here that simple faith in God, and love for one's fellow man, might be enough to secure salvation. Certainly, there is a sense of this idea in the fact that Jesus brought his teachings to the poor, to the dispossessed, to sinners, and to outcasts, and claimed that in the kingdom of God the current order of things would be reversed:

> How hard it is for the rich to enter the kingdom of God! Indeed, it is easier for a camel to go through the eye of a needle than for a rich man to enter the kingdom of God. (Luke 18:24–25)

Jesus advocated stringent ethical standards. Not only was it necessary to behave in accordance with God's wishes, it was also necessary to cultivate a character that was similarly devout. People had to eschew lust and hatred, as well as adultery and violence. Jesus's commitment to moral purity can been seen in his attitude towards divorce, which he equated with adultery.

This kind of moral perfectionism was linked to Jesus's eschatological views. He believed that the kingdom of God was imminent. It followed, therefore, that the injunction to moral purity was urgent in every possible sense. The fate of all people, Jew and Gentile alike, depended upon it.

Jesus of Nazareth is often portrayed as being the bearer of "good news" (which, in fact, is the meaning of the word "gospel"). This might sit uneasily with the demands that he placed upon his followers, but the crucial point is that he was offering salvation to every person. It was only necessary to accept the need for repentance, to embrace the Lord as savior, and salvation would be achieved. In a context where salvation had previously been possible only for a select few, this was a profoundly radical and welcome message. Indeed, it was precisely this that enabled St. Paul to bring the Christian message to the Gentiles, thereby facilitating the growth of Christianity as a world religion.

> But many who are first will be last, and many who are last will be first.
>
> Matthew 19:30

The Great Apostle

St. Paul

Paul of Tarsus, later St. Paul, was a pivotal figure in the emergence of Christianity. He was tireless in his attempts to spread the Gospel of Christ, and it was his insistence that the teachings of Christ be applied universally that encouraged the expansion of Christianity around the world.

Born: Ca. 10 CE, Tarsus
Importance: The first great apostle to the Gentiles
Died: Ca. 67 CE, Rome

St. Paul was not always a devotee of the Christian faith. Born Saul into a devout Jewish family, he spent the early part of his life persecuting Christians, often to their deaths. However, on the road between Jerusalem and Damascus, his life turned upside down when he had his famous conversion experience. According to the book of Acts:

> suddenly a light from heaven flashed around him. He fell to the ground and heard a voice say to him, "Saul, Saul, why do you persecute me?"
> "Who are you, Lord?" Saul asked.
> "I am Jesus, whom you are persecuting," he replied. "Now get up and go into the city, and you will be told what you must do." (Acts 9:3–5)

Paul was commissioned to take the message of the Gospel to Jews and Gentiles alike. In taking the Gospel to the Gentiles, he played a crucial role in the emergence of Christianity, which, in its earliest stages, was in effect a sect of Judaism. As a result, an argument emerged among the very first Christians about whether Gentile converts to Christianity should be required to follow established Jewish laws, particularly those concerning circumcision and diet.

10 11

In the face of opposition, Paul insisted that faith in Jesus Christ and purity of heart alone were enough to achieve righteousness. It was, he preached, clear that Gentiles should be allowed to participate as full members of the Christian body, regardless of whether they were circumcised or followed Jewish Law. This marked a crucial break with the ancient past of Israel and prepared the ground for the emergence of Christianity as a world religion. Some scholars suggest that in the absence of Paul's work among the Gentiles, Christianity would have remained just an offshoot of Judaism.

Although Paul stressed that salvation depended on faith, he did not believe that it did not matter how people behaved. Indeed, part of what he bequeathed to the future was the fairly stringent Christian moral code. For example, he insisted that believers

> Flee from sexual immorality. All other sins a man commits are outside his body, but he who sins sexually sins against his own body.
> (1 Corinthians 6:18)

He also denounced both divorce and homosexuality, the ramifications of which are still felt today. St. Paul's legacy can be seen in the reach of Christianity across the globe today. His message of inclusivity and acceptance paved the way for the development of Christianity as a major religion.

Apostles: In a general sense, an apostle is a person who preaches some specific idea, particularly Christianity. More specifically, the Apostles were the original twelve followers of Jesus Christ, who were enjoined to preach the gospel and spread the message of Christ.

Tertullian

Tertullian is recognized today as one of Christianity's greatest polemical authors, as well as a brilliant apologist for his faith. He is also considered exemplary as somebody willing to stand squarely behind his faith, even in the face of persecution.

Born: Ca. 155 CE, Carthage
Importance: A brilliant apologist and polemicist for the cause of Christianity
Died: after 220 CE, Carthage

He was a tough-minded and obdurate Christian. Nowhere was this more evident than in his attitude toward the fact that Christians under Roman rule were often persecuted for their beliefs:

It never happens without God willing it, and it is fitting — even at times necessary — for Him to do so . . . this is his winnowing fan which even now cleanses the Lord's threshing floor.

This uncompromising attitude is absolutely characteristic of his writings. The most important of these comprise his Christian apologetics, that is, his defence of Christianity against its critics. His great work is *Apologeticus* (197 CE), in which he takes on those unbelievers who seek in various ways to oppress Christians. He begins by issuing a challenge: if Christians are guilty of crimes, then their accusers should at least present evidence of their transgressions.

He goes on to point out that unbelievers have been guilty of the same crimes that Christians stand accused. He is similarly confrontational when he turns his attention to

> We say, and before all men we say, and torn and bleeding under your tortures, we cry out, "We worship God through Christ."
>
> Tertullian, *Apologeticus*

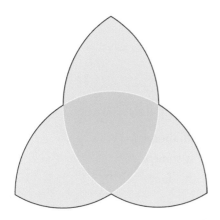

Left: Tertullian's description of the Holy Trinity as "one substance, three persons" has become the standard Christian understanding of the concept of God as simultaneously yet separately the Father, the Son, and the Holy Spirit.

the various Roman and pagan gods. They were all once men, he insists, and they haven't done anything since to warrant their being called gods. In contrast, Christians believe in just one Creator God, who is invisible, infinite, and to whom men bear witness. Moreover, Christians possess a divinely inspired testimony that is inscribed in their sacred books. He then explains that Jesus Christ, the son of God, performed miracles, was killed on the cross, and was subsequently resurrected.

Although known best for his apologetics, Tertullian has other historical significance. He was also the first Latin author to invoke the concept of the Christian Trinity. The formulation he employed, *una substantia, tres personae* ("one substance, three persons"), was to become the standard in Latin theology.

Tertullian embraced a moral code that was remarkable for its rigor. As a consequence, he was led to break from the Orthodox church, embracing the heretical Montanist movement, which stressed moral austerity, and the imminence of the end of world. However, even the Montanists lacked the rigor to satisfy him, and he eventually broke away to form his own sect, the Tertullianists.

Christianity

Christian Denominations

It is common to speak of Christianity, and the Christian Church, as if it were a single entity. The reality, of course, is very different. The Christian faith is characterized by disagreement and division.

The best known of its schisms is that between the Roman Catholic and Protestant denominations. This has its historical roots in the Reformation and the publication of Martin Luther's *95 Theses* (1517), which criticized Rome for the sale of indulgences to ensure the remission of punishment for sin. The Catholic Church had, he believed, lost sight of the original meaning of salvation, placing unwarranted emphasis on the possibility of attaining salvation through good works.

The controversy over indulgences was only one aspect of the divergence between Luther's ideas and Roman orthodoxy. Protestantism spread across much of Northern Europe, and although Luther had originally intended that his views would be only a corrective *within* the Catholic Church, the Lutheran movement quickly broke away entirely from Rome. The ramifications of this split are still evident. Most notoriously, the sectarian violence in Northern Ireland, though a complex phenomenon, is rooted in the historical division between Catholics and Protestants.

Not all denominational differences are this dramatic. In theological terms, it is possible for a denomination to move a long way from orthodox Christianity, yet still be considered part of the Christian family. Consider, for example, Jehovah's Witnesses. Established in Pittsburg in 1872, Jehovah's Witnesses believe variously, in contrast to most Christians that Christ died on a stake, not a cross; that we are currently in "end times"; that God will soon defeat Satan in a great battle of Armageddon; that this will be followed by a 1,000-year reign of Christ on earth; and that only a select 144,000 will go to heaven to rule with Christ.

Just how far apart it is possible to be in terms of beliefs, and yet still be considered part of the same religion, can be illustrated by comparing Jehovah's Witnesses to another Christian denomination — for example, Quakers. In contrast to the highly specified beliefs of the Witnesses, Quakers have little in the way of a formal creed. George Fox, the founder of Quakerism, was highly suspicious of theologians and stressed instead the possibility of a direct knowledge of God and divine truth. As a consequence, Quakers vary enormously in their specific beliefs, and it is even possible to find Quakers who do not believe in God at all.

If one looks at the totality of Christian denominations and sects, one is struck by the complexity of the situation. It is possible to identify, among others, Adventist, Baptist, Eastern Orthodox Church, European Free Church (for example, Quakers), Latter-Day Saint, Lutheran, Pentecostal, Methodist, Catholic, and Anglican groupings. What is it that defines the 2.1 billion people who make up these various denominations as being Christian? It is possible that there isn't any one belief that defines Christianity, but rather that it is a matter of "family resemblance" and sharing enough beliefs in common. Another view is that it is the doctrinal centrality of Jesus Christ, and the importance afforded to the example of his life, that constitutes Christian faith. Certainly, of the existing Christian denominations, nearly all of them — if not, in fact, all of them — disseminate what they understand to be the message of Christ.

HELIAS HIGH SCHOOL
LIBRARY
Jefferson City, MO

Christianity

Augustine

St. Augustine of Hippo is one of the most important fathers of the Christian church. His thoughts about free will, original sin, predestination, and God's grace had a profound effect on the development of Christianity.

Born: 354 CE, Tagaste, Numidia
Importance: After St. Paul, the most significant of the fathers of the Christian church
Died: 430 CE, Hippo Regius, Algeria

Augustine held a set of strict and stringent beliefs. He thought, for example, that babies who died unbaptized would not be admitted to heaven, but suffer eternal damnation from God in hell. He also believed that sex should be avoided unless absolutely necessary for the purposes of procreation, as sex involved the triumph of lustful urges, and therefore violated the requirement that virtuous people should at all times be in control of their own will.

Augustine's theology was linked to a specific view of Creation and the fall of man. He believed that when God created Adam, he had created him with free will and that Adam could have followed a path of righteousness by abstaining from sin. However, he chose not to and consequently fell into corruption. Mankind then inherited this "original sin." We therefore have no grounds for complaint if we end up in hell, because we are wicked and depraved to the core.

However, Augustine did not think that everybody would go to hell. Rather, by God's grace, a select few from among the baptized will be saved. However, there is a catch here. There is nothing that we can actually do to earn God's grace. We are depraved, and no number of good deeds will cancel this fact. However, God, by virtue of his goodness, chooses to bestow grace upon an elect few, and they, empowered to follow the ways of God, will upon their deaths go to heaven.

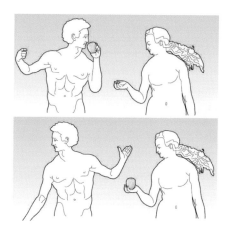

Left: Augustine thought that human beings had free will: Adam could have chosen to follow God's path and not eat the apple, but he chose to rebel against God and eat the apple. This "original sin" was then inherited by mankind.

There is something a little curious about Augustine's theology of predestination. Bertrand Russell pointed out in his great *History of Western Philosophy* (1946) that Augustine doesn't worry too much about the fact that God created mankind knowing that the vast majority are inevitably going to end up in hell. Yet he does worry about such details as the fact that the doctrine of original sin requires that the soul, the locus of sin, as well as the body, is inherited from the parents.

There is no denying Augustine's influence on Christian thinking. In his church history, Lutheran scholar Dr. Kurtz calls Augustine "the greatest, the most powerful of all the Fathers, him from whom proceeds all the doctrinal and ecclesiastical development of the West, and to whom each recurring crisis, each new orientation of thought brings it back." Still, the austerity and unforgiving nature of Augustine's theology make him a very difficult person to admire, even allowing for the fact that he lived in a time when different standards prevailed.

Pelagius

The teachings of Pelagius are no longer well known in Christian circles. However, in the first century CE his unorthodox views attracted a large following and ultimately resulted in his condemnation and excommunication. The source of his troubles were the ideas that he had about original sin and human free will, two of the most important and controversial areas in Christian theology.

Born: Ca. 354 CE, Britain
Importance: Questioned the idea of original sin and the necessity of divine grace for redemption
Died: not recorded, after 418 CE, possibly in Palestine

The concept of original sin is central to orthodox Christian thought. It holds that as a consequence of man's rebellion against God at the Fall (recorded in Genesis chapters two and three), sin is inherent to the human condition and can only be atoned for by the grace of God. Pelagius, however, did not accept the necessity of divine grace for redemption. He argued that we are not born already tainted by Adam's sin. Rather, we can choose by our own free will to live righteously and secure eternal life by our own efforts.

For Pelagius, these were not mere abstract speculations but went right to the heart of whether Christians can live morally worthy lives. He had been shocked at the moral degeneracy he had found in Rome when he traveled there at the end of the fourth century. He blamed this degeneracy on the effects of the Augustinian notion of divine grace. In particular, he was horrified by Augustine's famous prayer: "Grant what Thou commandest, and command what Thou dost desire."

Pelagius could not accept that grace was necessary in order to perform God's will. Such a conception, he thought, brings the whole moral order into danger. It suggests that human beings are not able to act righteously out of their own volition and that sin occurs because of unavoidable human weakness.

Pelagius insisted, in contrast, that humans have the ability to choose between good and evil. He advocated spiritual asceticism, in line with his Stoic leanings, as the means to attain moral perfection. However, he did not discount a role for God's grace altogether. He argued that grace is manifest in those characteristics that allow humanity to choose the path of righteousness: free will, conscience, and reason.

Pelagius's views were opposed by Augustine, who claimed to have identified nine teachings of the church that were denied by Pelagius. These included that death comes from sin, that infant baptism is necessary in order to clear original sin, that no good works are possible without God's grace, and that we confess that we are sinners not out of humility, but because it is true.

Pelagius disputed Augustine's account of his views. Despite this, he was condemned and excommunicated from the Catholic Church in 417 CE. Although Pelagius then disappeared from the historical record, the issues his work addressed remain central and controversial to this day. Original sin, free will, and divine grace are among the most important, contested, and complex ideas in Christian theology.

Divine grace: Christian theology holds that humans are "fallen." Grace refers to God's gift of unmerited salvation that allows for the possibility of human redemption. More generally, grace describes the love and mercy that God exhibits towards mankind.

Anselm of Canterbury

Anselm of Canterbury, later St. Anselm, believed that reason alone could be used to resolve theological debates. Specifically that it could prove the existence of God; establish that he has a triune nature (Father, Son, and Holy Spirit); demonstrate that the human soul is immortal; and show that scripture is inerrant.

Born: 1033, Aosta, Lombardy
Importance: Showed how it might be possible to demonstrate revealed truth using reason alone
Died: 1109, possibly Canterbury, England

Anselm did not, however, think that it was necessary to come to rational knowledge of God in order to believe in Him. Rather, it was precisely the other way around. He wished to make the truths of revelation transparent to reason. As he put it: "Unless I first believe, I shall not understand."

It is possible to get a sense of the way Anselm worked by considering an example from his work *The Fall of the Devil* (c. 1070). Anselm asks whether or not the devil had prior knowledge that he would fall. If he did have prior knowledge, then he either accepted what was going to happen or he didn't. If he accepted it, then he can't have had prior knowledge, because in the very act of acceptance he had already fallen. If he didn't accept it, then he would be grief stricken. However, this is impossible because the devil, prior to his fall, was sinless and therefore free of grief. Anselm concluded that it follows that the devil cannot have had prior knowledge of his fall.

This argument now seems rather arcane, but Anselm developed arguments of a similar kind that are still very much alive. His formulation in the *Proslogion* of the ontological proof of God is the classic example. It works like this:

1. God is defined as "that than which nothing greater can be conceived."

2. Things which exist in the mind — that is, the idea of God — might also exist in reality. In other words, there are two possibilities: God exists only in the mind or God exists in the mind and in reality.

3. Things which exist in the mind and in reality are greater than those things that exist just in the mind.

4. Let's assume that God exists only in the mind. We are then led into contradiction. We defined God as "that than which nothing greater can be conceived." But we have just seen that things which exist in the mind and in reality are greater than those things that exist just in the mind. Therefore, God cannot exist just in the mind.

It follows then:

5. God exists — both in the mind and in reality.

This argument has generated volumes of literature since it was first articulated nearly 1,000 years ago, and arguments concerning the ontological proof still continue. Anselm's reputation, however, does not depend on his arguments being correct. Instead, his legacy is that he showed that it was possible to employ reason to shed light on theological issues. This has led him to being labeled the Father of Scholasticism — the first great thinker, certainly in the Christian tradition, who attempted to secure the rational foundations of religious faith.

St. Thomas Aquinas

Many people think that religious belief depends largely upon faith, and that the revealed truths of religion are authoritative and brook no dissent. However, this begs the question that if reason has no part to play in religious belief, why did God create mankind with this faculty, and why has it been so successful as a means to knowledge in other fields of human endeavor? Thinking such as this led the great medieval theologian St. Thomas Aquinas to the view that it was desirable to reconcile faith and reason and to show that there are good reasons, independent of faith, for believing in the truth of the Bible.

Born: Ca.1225, Roccasecca, Italy

Importance: Showed how religious belief might be founded on reason

Died: 1274, Fossaunuova, Italy

Perhaps the best example of Aquinas's desire to work within the bounds of reason is to be found in his Five Ways (*quinque viae*). This work was his attempt to prove the existence of God on the basis of five philosophical arguments about motion, causation, contingency, perfection, and purpose. His Second Way, for instance, holds that the world is characterized by specific causal relations. If I hit a tennis ball with a racket, then the ball is set in motion by the racket, which in turn is caused to be moved by my arm, and so on. In this sequence of events, there is no uncaused cause. Rather, there are effects of antecedent causes, which then become causes themselves. The important point is that this backward chain of causality cannot continue forever. At some point, there must be an uncaused cause — the thing that started the whole chain of causes in the first place. Aquinas claimed that this uncaused cause is God.

One can see the exercise of reason in this argument. It proceeds by means of inference and logical deduction. However,

God → Big bang → Earth

Above: What caused the Big Bang? And was this cause itself caused? If Aquinas is right, at the beginning of the chain we must eventually find something that is not itself caused. This is God.

although it seems plausible at first sight, the argument is not decisive. It is not clear that a chain of causes cannot extend back indefinitely, and even if it cannot, there is no good reason to suppose that the uncaused, first cause will be the kind of thing we'd want to call God, and certainly not the Christian God — omnipotent, omniscient, and benevolent. Today it is generally accepted by theologians that Aquinas's Five Ways are not decisive in proving the existence of God. But they remain exemplary as demonstration of the way that reason can be used in order to support religious belief.

Aquinas did not believe that it would ever be possible to understand God fully through the use of reason, as he considered humans too limited for this. Indeed, the knowledge that we do attain comes to us through analogy and negation, that is, we know what God is not.

Aquinas was hugely influential. His followers, the Thomists, were central to the development of Christian theology. Most importantly, Aquinas showed that religious belief is not, and should not be, supported only by faith.

Christianity

The Jesuit

Ignatius of Loyola

Ignatius of Loyola founded the Jesuit order of the Catholic Church in 1534. The Jesuits played an active role in opposing the Protestant Reformation, and today the Jesuits are the largest male religious order in the Catholic Church, counting more than 20,000 people among their number.

Born: 1491, Loyola, Spain
Importance: The founder of the Society of Jesus (or Jesuits)
Died: 1556, Rome, Italy

Ignatius transformed his life during the period of months he spent in a cave in Manresa in 1522. His ascetic lifestyle is said to have caused him to have visions, one of which was the defining religious experience of his life. He never revealed the precise nature of this experience, but it seems that he thought that he had encountered God's true aspect. As a result, he came to see everything in a new light, and in particular was led to the conclusion that God is present in all things.

At about this time, he began to write *Spiritual Exercises* (1548), a collection of meditations, prayers, and intellectual activities. Ignatius described these exercises as

> every method of examination of conscience, of vocal and mental prayer . . . to prepare and dispose the soul to rid itself of all inordinate attachments; and after their removal, to seek and find God's will concerning the disposition of one's life for the salvation of the soul.

He developed these exercises on the basis of his understanding of scripture and also on the basis of direct spiritual experience. They were designed to help believers glorify God, and to lead them into a life dedicated to this purpose, and they engaged both the intellect and emotions to this effect.

Ignatius then embarked on a period of study with the aim of entering the priesthood. However, he got himself into trouble — and was arrested twice — for teaching people about religion without the necessary qualifications. This was during the Spanish Inquisition, which begain in 1478. At this time, any religious teacher, especially one such as Ignatius who had attracted a number of followers, was regarded with suspicion.

His followers included Francis Xavier, Peter Faber, Alfonso Salmeron, Diego Laynez, Nicholas Bobadilla, and Simon Rodrigues. In 1534, together with these six, Ignatius founded the Society of Jesus, whose members pledged to engage in whatever duties the Pope wished them to undertake.

The goal of the new religious order was the salvation of its own members (the Jesuits) and humanity as a whole. Ignatius was chosen to be the first Superior General of the Society of Jesus, and he dedicated the remainder of his life to directing the activities of the new society throughout the world.

Perhaps most significantly, Ignatius and the Jesuits were active in opposing the Protestant Reformation, playing an important part in the Counter-Reformation. The Jesuits urged believers to continue to obey both scripture and papal authority, with Ignatius himself going so far as to say

The Jesuits: A religious order of the Catholic Church, founded before the counterreformation in 1534. It emphasized obedience to scripture, the Pope, and Catholic doctrine. They focused on founding schools, converting non-Christians to Catholicism, and preventing the spread of Protestantism.

We should always be disposed to believe that that which appears white is really black, if the hierarchy of the Church so decides.

Martin Luther

Martin Luther is perhaps best known as the inspiration for the Protestant Reformation. His insistence on the primacy of scripture over papal authority was the beginning of a period of questioning that eventually led to a schism in the Catholic Church in the 1500s.

Born: 1483, Eisleben, Germany
Importance: His teachings inspired the Protestant Reformation
Died: 1546, Eisleben, Germany

As a young man, Martin Luther was unconvinced about the certainty of his own salvation. He felt himself to be a sinner in the presence of God. His inability to deal with this sense of unworthiness led him almost to hate the God he purportedly worshipped. Yet through intense study, he gained a new understanding of salvation that transformed his religious worldview.

It was the Christian orthodox view that one gained righteousness, perhaps through good works, in *conjunction* with God's help. Luther disagreed, arguing that righteousness is *granted* through faith. Salvation is not something that can be achieved. It is rather a gift of God's grace given through the life of Jesus Christ. This doctrine of justification (or salvation) underpins all of Luther's teaching. Luther wrote in his *Preface to the Epistle to the Romans* (1552)

> Faith is a living, daring confidence in God's grace, so sure and certain that a man can stake his life on it a thousand times.

This reworking of the idea of salvation put him into conflict with the Catholic Church. This was most notably evident on the publication of his *95 Theses* in 1517. In it, Luther denied the right of Rome to grant indulgences (a remission of punishment for sin) or pardons. His theses were widely read and found a receptive audience among the poor and among local civil authorities who suffered because of the transfer of funds to Rome. His argument against indulgences was straightforward: there is nothing in scripture to suggest that the Pope has the power to grant a remission of punishment. The crucial point here is that he favored scripture over papal authority, leading to the Reformation.

The indulgence controversy was by no means the extent of Luther's disagreement with Rome. For example, he also denied the ability of priests to mediate between individuals and God. By this he meant that the freedom of Christians resides in their redemption by the grace of God. What is required from them is that they spend their whole lives in God's service.

There is a temptation from a modern perspective to cheer Luther as he takes on the might of the Roman Catholic Church. However, he held views that are considered unacceptable by standards of modern morality. For example, he was a vehement opponent of Judaism, advising that people should set fire to synagogues and confiscate Jewish homes and money.

However, there is no denying his significance as a historical figure. Not only did he set the wheels of the Reformation in motion, but his teachings became the basis of the Lutheran Church, which in the present day counts a membership of some seventy million people.

The Reformation: A sixteenth-century movement intended to reform the Catholic Church, which resulted in the emergence of the Protestant faith across Western Europe. This in turn led to the Counter-Reformation, the reforms and structural changes implemented in Catholicism to halt the growth of Protestantism.

Creationism

The term "creationism" refers most commonly to the belief that the Earth was created by God as described in Genesis, the first book of the Bible. It is normally presented as an alternative to Darwin's theory of evolution, as an explanation for the existence of human life on earth. Many creationists therefore see themselves as opposing a scientific orthodoxy that is rooted in an unthinking metaphysical naturalism (the belief that all that exists is natural rather than supernatural).

Creationism in its modern form, largely a North American phenomenon, emerged in the eighteenth and nineteenth centuries, as science, and secularism more generally, began to encroach upon territory that had previously been the province of religion. In the United States, it was associated most significantly with the rise of Christian fundamentalism that occurred in the late nineteenth century. The impetus for the development of this movement was the perception on the part of conservative Protestants that Biblical authority was being undermined by rationalism and modernity. The teaching of Darwinism, in particular, was condemned in the movement's publication *The Fundamentals* as "the most deplorable feature of the whole wretched propaganda."

As the American fundamentalist movement grew, a lot of pressure was applied at state level, particularly in the South, in an attempt to curtail the teaching of evolution in schools. This led directly to the famous Scopes Trial of 1925, which saw John Scopes, a teacher, prosecuted for violating a Tennessee law banning the teaching of evolution. The trial featured a confrontation between William Jennings Bryan, a staunch antievolutionist, and Clarence Darrow, a noted defense lawyer.

Although Scopes lost the case, Darrow managed to humiliate Byran on the witness stand, and the event was subsequently considered a disaster for fundamentalism, Biblical inerrancy, and the creationist explanation of the origins of life.

The debate about creationism in America moved out of the public eye in the 1930s and 1940s, as Christian fundamentalism more generally came under pressure as modernity swept all before it. Indeed, in 1967 the Tennessee law banning the teaching of evolution was repealed. However, somewhat ironically, it was around this time that creationism, together (and not coincidentally) with Christian fundamentalism, began to reassert itself in the public and political sphere.

In its modern incarnation, creationism has a number of guises. These include young earth creationism, which asserts that the Earth, and life on it, was created a few thousand years ago, literally as described in Genesis; progressive creationism, which accepts most of the scientific account of evolution, but asserts that God intervened in the process; and, most recently, intelligent design, a movement that asserts that there are elements of the natural world best explained with reference to a designer (for example, the irreducible complexity of certain features of living organisms).

The various creationist movements retain an interest in affecting how science is taught in schools and in securing equal time for creationist accounts of the origins of human beings. However, though they have had limited success in states such as Kansas, where, for a brief period, evolution was eradicated from the state's science curriculum, they have suffered a number of defeats in court, including in 2005 when Judge John E. Jones III ruled that intelligent design is not science and is essentially religious in nature.

John Calvin

John Calvin, a sixteenth-century Protestant theologian of the Reformation, believed that humans are absolutely dependent upon God. Not only in the sense that God is the creator and ruler of all things, but also in that our destinies are absolutely in His hands.

Born: 1509, Noyon, Picardy, France
Importance: Articulated a theory of predestination that had an important impact on the formation of modern thought
Died: 1564, Geneva, Switzerland

Calvin accepted the Augustinian view that as a result of man's rebellion against God, humans are born sinful. The natural consequence of this is eternal damnation. However, Calvin argued that by his grace, God has chosen to be merciful to some and to predestine them for eternal salvation. These chosen people are the "elect." Unfortunately, there are also those, the "reprobates," whom God has not chosen to be merciful towards, and these people are destined to suffer the torment of eternal damanation in hell.

The important point is that there is nothing we can do to alter our destiny. According to Calvinist doctrine, it is entirely God's choice whether a person is saved or not. "Unconditional election" means that a member of the elect can never fall from grace, while a reprobate can never earn eternal salvation no matter how good a life she tries to lead.

God by his eternal and immutable counsel determined once for all those whom it was his pleasure one day to admit to salvation, and those whom, on the other hand, it was his pleasure to doom to destruction.

Calvin, *Institutes of the Christian Religion*

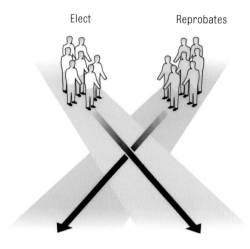

Elect   Reprobates

t: Calvin believed in the doctrine
ɔredestination: the "elect" were
stined for eternal salvation,
ile the "reprobates" would be
ɪdemned to eternal damnation.

The trouble with a theology of predestination is that it raises the question of how it is possible to know whether you are part of the elect or not. Calvin's response was that success in one's "calling" to God is a sign that one is part of the elect. That is, if you live a life that is wholly righteous by the light of the word of God, then you can take this as an indication that you are saved.

Although Calvin's theology is not disparate from other Reformers such as Martin Luther, his emphasis on predestination and the importance of success in one's calling is thought to have had a significant impact on the formation of the modern world. Sociologist Max Weber, for example, argued that the spark that led to the emergence of capitalism came from Calvinist ideas concerning hard work, thrift, and temperance.

Calvin had strong reservations about the capacity of the human mind to grasp the fundamental truths of religion except as these are revealed in the Bible. Rather, he stressed the importance of devoting oneself to worldly acts that would help usher in the reign of God on Earth. In this sense, Calvin's teachings are not so much a theology to be understood intellectually but rather a guide for Christian living.

John Wesley

The Holy Club, a religious studies group that John Wesley led at Oxford in the 1730s, was unlike most modern university societies. Such was the devotion of its members to methodical study and prayer that they attracted the nickname "the Methodists."

Born: 1703, Epworth, England
Importance: Founder of the Methodist movement
Died: 1791, London, England

The group's activities extended well beyond Oxford University. Its members visited the town's prison, teaching inmates how to read and helping them to find jobs. They also provided relief for the poor and visited workhouses with gifts of clothes and medicine.

At this early stage in his life, there was little that was distinctive about Wesley's theological position. In 1738, however, Wesley experienced a religious revelation. He became committed to the idea of the possibility of universal salvation.

The significance of Welsey's revelation will not be apparent without some awareness of the ideas of John Calvin. Calvinism holds that salvation is a gift from God that will be granted only to an elect few, and nothing the elect or non-elect can do will change their fate: it is all predestined.

Wesley's revelation, which led him to embrace a form of "Arminianism" (named after Joseph Arminius), was that by faith in Jesus Christ, and by faith alone, it is possible, by the grace of God, to achieve

I felt I did trust in Christ, Christ alone, for salvation; and an assurance was given me that He had taken away my sins, even mine, and saved me from the law of sin and death.

Wesley, *Journal*

salvation. This is a possibility open to everybody. Salvation is not restricted to the elect few.

Having come to this realization, Wesley became evangelical about his calling. He preached directly to the people, soon under the auspices of Methodist societies for which he had written a set of rules. His sermons became famous, and often elicited extreme reactions. For example, the miners of Kingswood, England, were reported to have broken down in tears on hearing his message. His endeavors, however, were not appreciated by everybody: the established church in particular saw him as a dangerous rabble-rouser.

Though it is well known that Wesley opposed the slave trade, it would not be true to portray him as a political revolutionary. Historians often argue that his ideas — and Methodism, more generally — helped to keep the working class quiescent during the difficult period of the French revolution and the Napoleonic wars. However, it is also true that many early Socialists had sympathy with the universal impulse behind his message; specifically, the idea that salvation is open to everybody, and that all men are equal in the eyes of God. Indeed, Morgan Phillips, a leading British Labour Party politician in the twentieth century, said that Socialism in Britain owed more to Methodism than it did to Marxism.

Methodism: An eighteenth-century Protestant movement that originated in Britain and spread through the world thanks to missionary activity. It sought to revitalize the church, focusing on a methodical approach to the scriptures, and the idea of salvation through faith as opposed to predestination.

Blaise Pascal

Blaise Pascal, the great seventeenth-century polymath, is best known in the religious field for his famous "wager," which attempts to demonstrate that belief in God is rational.

Born: 1623, Clermont-Ferrand, France

Importance: The author of the wager named after him — Pascal's Wager

Died: 1662, Paris

On the night of November 23, 1654, Pascal had a conversion experience, and religion became the dominant force in his life. His experience was so profound that he recorded it on a piece of parchment which he then had sewn into his coat, carrying it with him for the rest of his life.

After this experience Pascal, who had previously concerned himself largely with mathematics and physics, turned increasingly to writing on religion. His *Lettres Provinciales* (1656–1657) was an attack on the views of the Catholic order of Jesuits. In essence, he accused them of expediency in their theological and moral outlook. They were, he claimed, happy to sacrifice scriptural accuracy for political gain.

Pascal's wider theological views showed the influence of Augustine. He was committed to the view that only by the grace of God can people be redeemed. In his view, God's grace is such that those people he had blessed will always choose to follow his path. However, Pascal also believed in predestination; that is, the idea that salvation is preordained. Therefore, there is nothing specifically that the individual can do to attain salvation. Either God will make his presence felt or he will not.

This belief makes it slightly paradoxical that Pascal spent the final years of his life writing an apologia for Christianity. This was pieced together after his death as *Pensées* (1669). It is in this work that one finds Pascal's famous wager about the existence of God.

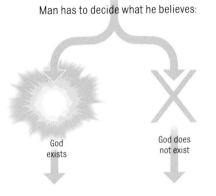

Man has to decide what he believes:

God exists

God does not exist

Left: Pascal's wager is an attempt to persuade people that believing in God is rational.

If this is true we could gain a lot; if this is false we lose nothing.

If this is true we lose nothing; if this is false we lose a lot.

He argued that either God exists or he does not and that we have to decide one way or another on this unavoidable existential dilemma. If he doesn't exist, we lose little by thinking he does; if he does exist, we stand to gain a lot by believing this, and to lose a lot by thinking that he doesn't. It therefore makes sense to wager that he does exist and to act accordingly.

The wager is not an argument for the existence of God. It is, rather, an argument for the *rationality* of belief in God. It was aimed primarily at people unsure whether God exists — people who are skeptical, but interested. It does, however, sit uneasily with his view of predestination. Pascal anticipated the criticism that trying to persuade people of the efficacy of religious belief is strange, if it is true that their belief is not constitutive of salvation. His response was that God might choose to do his work through other people, so it was his duty to attempt to bring people to faith.

Although he is best known for his wager, Pascal's intellectual reach was broad, and his scientific and mathematical work is just as impressive as his religious apologetics.

Christianity

George Fox

George Fox is remembered as an inspiring personality who sparked the emergence of a new religious movement: the Quakers. A core belief of the Quakers is that some small part of God exists in every person, and therefore there is potential for goodness in all. The movement has a long history of pacifism and civil rights activities and was involved in the abolition of slavery.

Born: 1624, Fenny Drayton, England

Importance: Founder of the Society of Friends (Quakers)

Died: 1691, London, England

Fox was not impressed with the clergy of seventeenth-century England. In his late teens, he described them as "miserable comforters" who made his troubles worse by variously offering him tobacco, shouting at him for stepping on a plant, and suggesting bloodletting as a cure for his diseased mind. Confirmation that his disdain was justified came one Sunday morning directly from God:

> The Lord opened in me an understanding, that being educated at Oxford or Cambridge was not enough to fit and qualify men to be ministers of Christ.

Fox is talking here about a direct apprehension, divinely inspired, of a religious truth. The consequences that flowed from his awareness of this possibility were many. Most particularly, it meant that it was not necessary to turn to the established church and its ministers to come to know God and his desires for the world. Fox experienced a series of revelations: God does not reside in the religious buildings that men have built for him, the established clergy do not have true faith, and that it was his personal calling to bring people to the spirit of Christ that was within them. "These things I did not see by the help of man, nor by the letter, though they are written in the letter, but I saw them in the light of the Lord Jesus Christ, and by his immediate Spirit and powers . . ."

Fox began the task of bringing his message to the people of England in 1647. His early devotees were nicknamed Quakers, as they were said to tremble or quake with religious zeal. He taught of the evils of established religion and the benefits of his own doctrine of direct revelation by means of an "inner light." He also preached a number of other more specific beliefs, including an eschewal of religious authority and opposition to war and slavery.

George Fox did not endear himself to the authorities by his activities. He readily offended religious leaders by publicly contradicting them and refusing to engage in religious ritual or pay tithes. He was imprisoned on eight different occasions during his lifetime. However, this did not prevent his Quaker church from growing in size and getting its organizational basis sorted out. Fox responded to his difficulties by lobbying for a change of law that would allow freedom of religious expression. The Act of Toleration was passed in 1689, shortly before his death.

The Quakers, now officially called the Religious Society of Friends, are still going strong. Many of George Fox's original teachings retain their significance in Quaker circles.

The Quakers: Originating in seventeenth-century England due to dissatisfaction with the existing religious order, the Quakers advocated pacifism and the right to live and worship according to individual beliefs and inner revelations. Among the various branches of Quakerism there are few central tenets common to all.

Søren Kierkegaard

Søren Kierkegaard, one of the great philosophers of the nineteenth century, denied that it was possible to make God and the Christian faith transparent to reason. He believed that they are beyond rational understanding.

Born: 1813, Copenhagen, Denmark

Importance: Denied that faith and the Christian religion could be understood rationally

Died: 1855, Copenhagen, Denmark

Specifically, he argued that the sphere of religion is constituted by a "leap of faith" that takes it outside the domain of rationality. The Christian's worship of the God-man Jesus is paradoxical. It is simply not possible to appeal to rational argument or empirical evidence to justify such a belief. The only thing available is passionate commitment. In his book *Fear and Trembling* (1843), Kierkegaard detailed what this might mean for ethics by analyzing the biblical story of Abraham and Isaac.

In Genesis, the first book of the Bible, God orders Abraham to kill his son Isaac. According to Kierkegaard, to obey this command necessitates behavior that is completely outside the domain of normal morals. It requires a suspension of the ethical in the service of a higher goal (*telos*). He illustrates this by comparing the situation of Abraham to that of a "tragic hero."

Consider the following scenario: A military commander knows that if he wants to avoid losing a battle, then he must send a battalion of soldiers to certain death. The battalion includes his son. This constitutes a desperate moral dilemma, but one that it is nevertheless possible to look at rationally. Whatever the commander decides, he'll be able to offer a justification that other people will understand. The situation is not the same with Abraham. He must simply follow an order that comes to him from above, and which will have a consequence that is unthinkable in the terms of normal moral discourse. Not only can he not justify his actions to other people, he cannot even tell himself a story to explain why it is required of him. All that counts is his absolute commitment to a subjective, felt relationship with God.

Religious faith then is not an easy option. Indeed, Kierkegaard argued that proper religious faith can be achieved only with difficulty. Of course, this raises the question of why one would choose it at all. He answered that it is only by religious faith that individuals can avoid despair and can find their true selves in the freedom which, paradoxically, dependence upon a transcendent being brings.

There are problems with highlighting the irrationality of religious belief. Not least there is the possibility that the core of irrationality which lies at the heart of Kierkegaard's thinking about religion could all too easily transmute into a kind of nihilism or even fascism. After all, as Voltaire made clear, many terrible things have been justified on the basis of appeals to faith (and Kierkegaard himself had some pretty reactionary social views).

Nevertheless, Kierkegaard's importance as a religious thinker and philosopher is without question. Although he was not recognized as a great thinker during his lifetime, with the emergence of existentialism in the twentieth century, which placed the individual at the center of things, the originality and importance of his work — particularly as it fused philosophical and religious themes — became fully appreciated.

Faith: For Kierkegaard, faith is not a matter of regurgitating church dogma. It is a matter of individual subjective passion, which cannot be mediated by the clergy or by human artefacts. Faith is the most important task to be achieved by a human being, because only on the basis of faith does an individual have a chance to become a true self.

Gustavo Gutierrez

Gutierrez is the author of groundbreaking work developing what he called "liberation theology." He argued that theology should reflect the contemporary social context to which it was addressed, rather than remaining unchanged through time.

Born: 1928, Lima, Peru

Importance: Articulated the definitive statement of liberation theology

The foundational claim of liberation theology is that theology arises in and is addressed to specific historical contexts and circumstances. Theology, according to Gutierrez, should always be "a critical reflection on Christian praxis [action] in light of the Word." It should be thoroughly immersed in the social context of faith and ready to meet the challenges of contemporary life.

In contrast to many orthodox theologians who see their discipline as relatively disengaged from the political and social world, Gutierrez insisted that social issues are central and that there are historical realities to be examined through theological practice.

Gutierrez's radical impulse stemmed partly from his experience of the abject poverty suffered by the dispossessed in many parts of South America. It was also motivated by his Christianity. He believed that the Christian faith requires that one actively pursues justice in the social and political sphere. Theology is directly bound up with the

. . . [the] theological moment is one of critical reflection from within, and upon, concrete historical praxis, in confrontation with the word of the Lord as lived and accepted in faith . . .

Gutierrez, *The Power of the Poor in History*

need to change the world for the better. This is a theology that tries to be part of the process through which the world is transformed, rather than being only reflective.

Gutierrez argued that the struggle for liberation was integrally linked to a striving for salvation. In his seminal work *A Theology of Liberation* (1973), he identified three aspects of liberation — from economic deprivation and exploitation, from fatalism, and from sin — enabling men and women to open up to God.

The advantage of insisting that these three aspects of liberation are part of a single process of salvation is that it is realistic in terms of the harsh circumstances that people confront. Rather than seeing salvation as being a purely spiritual matter, a matter of a personal relationship with God, it recognizes that this relationship is bound up with particular historical conditions.

Liberation theology has endured criticism from a number of sources. Particularly, it is argued that its focus tends to be more on political liberation than Christian theology. Specific allegations include that liberation theologians are apologists for violence and that they have a fondness for Marxist concepts that are incompatible with the message of Christianity.

It is perhaps too early to discern how history will view liberation theology, but it is fair to say that Gutierrez's *A Theology of Liberation* was one of the most important theological works of the twentieth century.

Liberation theology: A combination of Christian theology and political activism that advocates ideas of social justice and human rights. It examines religious theory in light of the current social and political context, in an attempt to liberate the poor and oppressed. It was particularly influential in Latin America.

Deism

Deism is the concept that it is possible to come to know the existence of God through the use of reason alone. According to this understanding, revelation plays no part in our knowledge of God. The term has also become associated with the idea that God created the Universe and then disappeared, allowing the Universe to run according to its own laws.

A deist of the second kind will also be a deist of the first kind as an absent God has no use for revelation. However, there is no reason why a deist of the first kind should be a deist of the second kind. Deism is entirely consistent with the idea of a personal God, present in the Universe and in the lives of human beings. It only insists that one comes to knowledge of this fact by the use of reason.

Deism came to prominence in England in the latter part of the seventeenth century on the back of increasing confidence in the power of science and reason. Its first exponent was Edward Herbert, who argued that right from the beginning of time man has possessed a number of God-given, innate religious ideas, including a disposition to believe in a supreme being, a need to worship him (most efficaciously by living a life of piety and virtue), a belief in the afterlife, and the idea that it will be characterized by rewards and punishments depending on how you lived your life. According to Herbert, these ideas lie at the heart of all religious devotion, constituting a "natural religion" that is possible to grasp by means of reason.

The deistic thinkers following Herbert, such as Anthony Collins and Matthew Tindal, tended to accept Herbert's contention that proper religious belief has to be rooted in reason, and they rejected the idea that sacred books revealed religious truths. This, of course, raises the question as to what would count as evidence for God's existence at all. The answer tended to refer to the ordered nature of the Universe. Voltaire, the great French deist, argued that the Universe displayed the marks of divinity in the order and regularity which Isaac Newton had so successfully explained.

The deists were resolutely opposed to religious extremism. Voltaire fought a one-man campaign against what he saw as the violent excesses of the Catholic Church of this period. The deist commitment to moderation was rooted in their advocacy of reason as a way to religious belief. If there is such a thing as a "natural religion," then every person has the ability to draw upon it, negating the need for exclusivity and intolerance.

> For as God has made us rational Creatures, and Reason tells us, that 'tis his Will, that we act up to the Dignity of our Natures; so 'tis Reason must tell when we do so.
>
> Matthew Tindal

Deism survives to this day, but in a truncated form. Its troubles turned out to be in the detail of its message. Deists were never able to agree which religious beliefs were supported by reason and the idea that there are elements of religious belief that are universal was falsified as historical and anthropological knowledge increased.

Muhammad

Muhammad, the great Prophet of the Muslim faith, was the historical founder of Islam. However, within the Islamic tradition itself, his life and work are seen as the culmination of the one true religion, previously imperfectly instantiated in the Abrahamic religions of Judaism and Christianity.

Born: 570 CE, Mecca
Importance: Founded the
Islamic religion
Died: 632 CE, Medina

Muhammad's core religious ideas, set down in the Qur'an, and believed to be the inspired word of God relayed to him by the Angel Gabriel, are not very different from those ideas characteristic of Judaism and Christianity. He taught that there is one eternal God (Allah), that there is no other God but him. He is omnisicent (all-knowing), omnipotent (all-powerful), beneficent, and just.

It is the duty of all people to worship and serve the one God, to live moral lives, and to seek the betterment of humankind. It was Muhammad's belief that humans were falling well short of this ideal. In particular, they were guilty of the sin of polytheism — of worshiping more than one God — and thereby failing to accord to God the exclusivity of devotion that is his right. For example, Christians had turned Jesus into a kind of God, and Arab polytheists had ascribed divinity to various angels. Muhammad's response was to insist that there is only one God and to preach of punishment in the afterlife for deviating from the path of righteousness.

Muhammad taught a set of highly prescribed rules governing the religious lives of his followers. His followers paid heed to these rules, integrating them into their daily practice. In his last impassioned sermon in 632 CE, he urged the followers to

Worship Allah, say your five daily prayers, fast during the
month of Ramadan, and give your wealth in Zakat. Perform
Hajj if you can afford to. You know that every Muslim is the
brother of another Muslim. You are all equal. Nobody has
superiority over another except by piety and good action.
Remember, one day you will appear before Allah and answer
for your deeds.

Muhammad articulated his message in the face of considerable
opposition. Consequently, the idea of struggle (jihad) is prominent
in the Qur'an. Scholars are divided as to the precise nature of
jihad — its limits and against whom it may be waged. However, it
is clear that in certain circumstances, particularly (and perhaps
only) where believers have been driven from their lands, the
Qur'an sanctions violence against unbelievers:

fight in the way of Allah with those who fight against you
. . . Kill them wherever you find them and drive them out
from which they drove you out.

The political aspects of Muhammad's ideas are clear
throughout the Qur'an. He sides with the oppressed, insisting that
God is on the side of justice, and he condemns material inequality,
commanding that all Muslims should give alms to the poor.
Indeed, the Qur'an itself can be read as a political tract; as
Michael Cook points out, it has a distinctive vocabulary of
monotheistic politics, the theme of which "is quite literally
revolution, the triumph of believers against the pervasive
oppression of unbelief."

Ali

Ali ibn Abi Talib (commonly shortened to "Ali"), the cousin of Muhammad, was, at the time of the Prophet's death, his closest living relative. This led some among the original Islamic community to the view that he should become the first Muslim caliph. His supporters also believed that this was Muhammad's desire: evidence for this was the fact that Muhammad had presented Ali to the close circle accompanying him on his final journey to Medina, advising that "Everyone whose patron I am, also has Ali as their patron."

Born: Ca. 599 CE, Mecca, Saudi Arabia

Importance: The inspiration for the emergence of Shia Islam.

Died: Ca. 661 CE, Kufa, Iraq

However, the majority of the original Muslim community, dissenting from this view, elected Abu Bakr as the first caliph. This, however, was not the end of the matter. Although Ali, desperate to avoid civil war, assented to Abu Bakr's leadership, he did not depart from his view that the Muslim community should be led by a direct male descendent of Muhammad.

Ali got his chance at leadership after the assassination of the third caliph, Uthman, in 656. This had plunged the city of Medina, at that time the center of the Islamic world, into chaos. Ali's supporters, known as Shi'is or shi'at Ali, urged him to the leadership, and although he was reluctant (it is said for fear of seeming to profit from Uthman's death), he succeeded to the position, becoming the Fourth "Rightly Guided Caliph" (for which he is still revered by all Muslims).

Ali's period of leadership, however, was characterized by internecine violence and civil war. His commitment to the idea that the Muslim community should be led only by (male) relatives of the Prophet aggravated an already tense situation. Indeed, the culture of intertribal bickering that Muhammad had sought to eradicate reappeared on the scene. Two prominent companions of Muhammad, Talha and al Zubayr, backed by Muhammad's widow, Aisha, led a rebel army against Ali, before being defeated at the Battle of the Camel (so called because Aisha chose to watch the unfolding events from a palanquin perched on a camel's back).

The most significant confrontation of Ali's leadership, however, was with Mu'awiya Ummayad, Uthman's cousin, the governor of Damascus. This resulted in a prolonged military standoff, with neither side able to claim decisive victory. Ali sought a compromise, but by this point he was losing both popular support and territory. In the end, controlling little more than central and southern Iraq among the occupied territories, he was assassinated in the Kufa mosque in 661 by a disaffected supporter from the breakaway Khariji faction.

After Ali's death, his followers split from other Muslims and became known as Shiites. According to the Shia, Ali has the status of "Friend of Allah" — next to Muhammad — and is at the center of many of the differences between Shia and Sunni Islam.

Abu Bakr

The death of the Prophet Muhammad on June 8, 632 CE brought with it the problem of who should succeed him as leader of the nascent Muslim community (*ummah*). The matter was settled in favour of Abu Bakr, a close advisor to Muhammad, at a meeting in the Saqifat Bani Sa'ida (a roofed building used by the tribe of Sa'ida).

Born: 573 CE, Mecca, Saudi Arabia

Importance: The first Muslim caliph

Died: 634 CE, Medina, Saudi Arabia

In many ways, Abu Bakr was the obvious choice. Tradition records that he was "a pious man with no aggressive traits" who had begun the process of piecing together the Qur'an, and that he was also a military genius. He is said to have been the first person after the Prophet's own family to convert to Islam. Muhammad clearly had a high opinion of him, dubbing him al-Siddiq, meaning "the one who always speaks the truth." Moreover, in the last few days before the Prophet's death, Abu Bakr had led the prayers, which was taken by some as an indication that he was the preferred choice as leader.

However, his elevation to the position of caliph sparked a rift within the Muslim community that still exists. While Sunni Muslims accept Abu Bakr's succession as legitimate, the Shia believe that the first caliph should have been Ali, Muhammad's closest blood relative. These contrary views are reflected in different versions of the events at Saqifah. The Sunni view is simply that the associates of Muhammad gathered together and then, after much discussion, decided upon Abu Bakr as the leader. The Shia view, in contrast, is that Abu Bakr and Umar conspired to seize leadership of the Muslim community from Ali, the Prophet's rightful heir. They point out that Ali, and other close members of Muhammad's family, were preparing the Prophet's body for burial while the leadership meeting was taking place. Furthermore, they claim that the meeting was not announced, and that it therefore attracted only a small number of Muslims who were not representative of the community as a whole.

Abu Bakr's leadership was eventually accepted by Ali. Abu Bakr proved himself to be an adept military leader and is credited with having eliminated any remaining opposition to Islam within Arabia. He was, nevertheless, obliged to put down several revolts during his caliphate, and during a fraught period between 632 and 633, in what became known as the Ridda Wars (or Wars of Apostasy), he conducted a series of military campaigns in order to defeat a number of "false prophets."

Once Abu Bakr had suppressed internal dissent within Arabia, he embarked upon a war of conquest. Some scholars argue that this was motivated by a desire to consolidate the caliphate's control over the region's Arabic-speaking powers. What is certainly true is that Abu Bakr initiated a period of rapid Islamic expansion that would, within a hundred years, result in one of the world's biggest-ever empires.

Caliph: The title of the leader of the Islamic community, and particularly those who immediately succeeded Muhammad (the four "rightly guided" caliphs). Although caliphs are religious leaders, they do not disseminate dogma, since the truth of Islam had been completed with Muhammad.

Shia Islam and Sunni Islam

Islam is characterized by a number of divisions, the most important of which is that between the Sunni and the Shia. This split has its origins in an argument about who should have succeeded the Prophet Muhammad as the first Muslim caliph (leader). Shia Muslims believe that it should have been Ali, Muhammad's closest living relative.

Thus, the Shia declaration of faith holds that

> There is no god but Allah, Muhammad is the Messenger of Allah, Ali is the Friend of Allah. The Successor of the Messenger of Allah and his first Caliph.

In fact, Abu Bakr became the first caliph, a decision supported by Sunni Muslims, partly on the grounds that he had led prayers in the last few days before Muhammad's death, indicating that he was the Prophet's preferred choice.

Ali did eventually succeed to the caliphate some twenty-four years after Muhammad's death, when the third caliph Uthman was murdered. His rule, however, was relatively brief. Mu'awiya succeeded to the caliphate, and then on his death his son Yazid declared himself caliph. This prompted Ali's son Hussein to lead an army against Yazid, but, greatly outnumbered, he and his men were massacred at the battle of Karbala. Hussein's struggle against Yazid, and his martyr's death, remain an important theme in Shia Islam.

The direct hereditary line to Muhammad ended in 873, when the twelfth Shia Imam, Muhammad al-Mahdi, vanished shortly after inheriting the title. Shias believe that he did not die, but rather went into occultation (hiding), from which he will return at the end of the world to usher in a reign of justice.

Both Sunnis and Shias agree that central to Islam are its Five Pillars: the Testimony of Faith, Ritual Prayer, the Giving of Alms, Fasting, and the Hajj, or Pilgrimage to Mecca. However, the two groups interpret some parts of the Qur'an differently, and the Shias have different hadith. Perhaps more significantly, Shia Islam is characterized by a strong theme of martyrdom that is absent from Sunni Islam. Thus, for example, the struggle of Ayatollah Khomeini and his followers during the Iranian revolution has been portrayed to great effect as analogous to Hussein's struggle at the battle of Karbala.

Hadith: Hadith are traditions relating to the words and deeds of Muhammad and are regarded as important tools for determining the Muslim way of life.

Many Islamic scholars have encouraged unity amongst Muslims. Most notably, Sheikh Shatoot, of the eminent al-Azhar Sunni theological school in Cairo, issued a fatwa in 1959 which proclaimed: "The Shia is a school of thought that is religiously correct to follow in worship as are other Sunni schools of thought."

Ibn al-Shafi'i

Ibn al-Shafi'i is generally considered to be the greatest of the original founders of the four distinct schools of Islamic law (Sharia) that remain dominant today — the Hanifi, Maliki, Shafi'i, and Hanbali schools. His ideas were influenced by his engagement with existing law laid down by his predecessors and contemporaries, and then were developed and formalized by his followers.

Born: 767 CE, Gaza, Palestine
Importance: Probably the greatest of the early Sharia jurists
Died: 820 CE, Egypt

Early in his life, Ibn al-Shafi'i came under the influence of Malik ibn Anas, the founder of the Maliki school of jurisprudence. However, he disagreed with his onetime teacher about the religious significance of the Sunnah — the practices of the original Islamic community — as it was instantiated in the law and religious practices of Medina, the second holy city of Islam. He argued that it was not safe to rely on the example of just one city, emphasizing instead the significance of the hadith — the reports of the sayings and doings of the Prophet Muhammad — as the source of Islamic law.

However, al-Shafi'i did not believe that the hadith could simply be assumed to be authentic. Rather, it was necessary to ensure that each hadith was supported by a chain of continuity, comprising devout Muslims, leading back to the time of Muhammad. It was as a result of this demand for historical accuracy that Islamic scholars began to consider which hadith were true and which were not.

Ibn al-Shafi'i's view was that Islamic law was to be derived from the example of the Prophet Muhammad as exemplified in his words and deeds, and that it was the duty of every Muslim to live a life as close to that of the Prophet as possible. He did allow

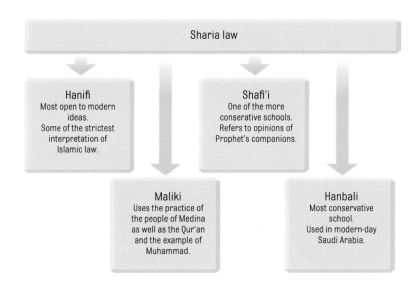

```
┌─────────────────────────────────────────────────────┐
│                     Sharia law                        │
└─────────────────────────────────────────────────────┘
```

Hanifi
Most open to modern ideas.
Some of the strictest interpretation of Islamic law.

Shafi'i
One of the more conserative schools.
Refers to opinions of Prophet's companions.

Maliki
Uses the practice of the people of Medina as well as the Qur'an and the example of Muhammad.

Hanbali
Most conservative school.
Used in modern-day Saudi Arabia.

Above: Sharia law is divided into four schools: Hanifi, Maliki, Shafi'i, and Hanbali. Each school has its own distinct teachings and beliefs.

for two other sources of Islamic law, which played a secondary role: *qadis* — reasoning by analogy in order to develop new laws from existing laws (allowing Islamic law to be sensitive to modern conditions); and *imja* — the consensus of a community: as God would not allow an entire Muslim community to be mistaken in all aspects, a commonly accepted custom could be accepted as a proper Islamic principle.

Ibn al-Shafi'i's work established a framework by which a systematized Islamic law might be developed. The work of the great jurists who had preceded him, such as Malik ibn Anas and Abu Hanifah, had resulted in schism and conflict because it relied on juristic speculation and was subject to the influence of their particular local situations. Al-Shafi'i's approach largely circumvented these problems and provided a model for the development of a relatively unified Islamic law.

Ibn Sina

Ibn Sina, better known in the Western world as Avicenna, developed systematic theories of being and God that relied heavily on the insights of Neoplatonist thinkers in the Islamic tradition such as al-Farabi. To the uninitiated, his theories seem strange and otherworldly, yet he is considered one of the greatest thinkers of the pre-Modern period.

Born: 980 CE, Bukhara, Iran

Importance: Combined Hellenistic philosophy with Islamic religious themes

Died: 1037 CE, Hamadan, Iran

It is possible to get a sense of his thought by considering his proof of the existence of God. Following in the traditions of Aristotle, Ibn Sina argued that existence is either necessary or merely possible. Roughly speaking, something exists necessarily if there is no possible world in which it does not exist. Something possibly, or contingently, exists if there is a possible world where it does not exist. We know that the world of our everyday experience is full of non-necessary entities — things are coming into being and then ceasing to exist all of the time. Ibn Sina's argument is that all this contingent stuff ultimately presupposes something that necessarily exists. Otherwise, given that it need not exist, there is nothing to explain why it does exist. In the end, there has to be some entity that necessarily exists, which contains the ground of its own existence, to function as the essential cause of all contingent existence. This is God.

This argument is fairly complex, but not particularly strange. His conception of God, and God's relation to the cosmos, however, is a different matter. Ibn Sina followed what is known as the "emanationist" view in arguing that the Universe was not created *ex nihilo* at a particular moment in time, but rather that it exists as a matter of necessity, emanating in its variety of forms

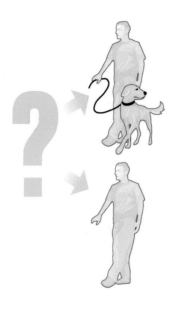

Left: Dogs might, or might not, exist in any particular world. They are contingent entities. Ultimately, all contingent entities must be created by a necessary entity. This is God.

from God's divine nature. To put this another way, God is the One, the pure intellect, upon which all of reality depends, and to which it is connected via logical relations.

This idea of God, and God's relation to the cosmos, played a large role in Ibn Sina's wider philosophical speculations. For example, he argued that our knowledge of the world is ultimately dependent upon God. He invoked something he called the "Active Intellect," a kind of higher mind directly connected to God, as the locus of human knowledge. He claimed that people vary in their capacity to gain knowledge depending upon their ability to come into conjunction with this Active Intellect. Prophets do very well; the impure and irreligious, not so well.

Ibn Sina's attempt to marry Hellenistic philosophy with Islamic religious themes was not uncontroversial. In particular, his approach came under pressure from those such as al-Ghazali who claimed that it robbed God of agency, turning him into something different from the God of the Qur'an. Nevertheless, he remains to this day a much admired figure in the Islamic world, particularly for his medical writings, but also for his contribution to philosophical and religious thought.

Al-Ghazali

Abu Hamid al-Ghazali, known in his own time as "the proof of Islam," is perhaps the first great specifically Muslim intellectual. His work in synthesizing philosophy, theology, jurisprudence, and Sufism (the mystic tradition of Islam) aimed to specify the proper relation between humans and God, providing a justification for Islamic ritual and practice.

Born: 1058, Tus, Iran
Importance: Integrated Sufism into the orthodox Islamic worldview
Died: 1111, Tus, Iran

If there were a single impulse motivating this project, it was the thought that though it might seem possible to know a lot *about* God by making use of established theological and philosophical methods, it isn't possible to *know* God, to have a direct experience of him, in this way. In his eleventh-century work *The Incoherence of the Philosophers*, al-Ghazali was heavily critical of those Islamic philosophers, such as Ibn Sina, who believed that it was possible to arrive at religious truths through the mechanism of Aristotelian reason.

In line with his Sufism, he believed instead that in a certain mystical state it is possible to gain a glimpse of the divine:

> I apprehended clearly that the mystics are men who had real experiences, not men of words. . . . What remained for me was not to be attained by oral instruction and study, but only by immediate experience and by walking in the mystic way.

The possibility of a direct knowledge of God is predicated upon the spiritual, or divine, qualities of the human soul. In the normal course of events, however, such knowledge is corrupted by a too powerful love of the material world. The purpose of prayer and religious ritual, then, is to redeem the soul, opening it

Above: The doctrine of the "Golden Mean" holds that any given virtue lies between two extremes, one involving deficiency and the other excess.

Thus, the virtue of courage lies between cowardice (deficiency) and rashness (excess).

up to the possibility of divine communication. The rules that al-Ghazali laid down in this respect were quite precise. He drew upon the Aristotelian concept of the "Golden Mean," which holds that humans will behave well if they avoid both excess and inappropriate moderation in their behavior. Good Muslims, therefore, should eschew unlawful and culpable behavior, such as that motivated by anger, greed, and the love of material possessions. In their place, enabled by an adherence to the Sharia laws concerning food, hygiene, sleep, prayer, and the like, Muslims should embrace virtues such as love (of God and others through God), temperance, wisdom, and justice. In this way, it would be possible for them to get into the state necessary for a proper approach to God.

Al-Ghazali was able to show that the restrictions and practices of Islam were not simply arbitrary constraints but had meaning and purpose. He also caused a fundamental shift in the nature of Islamic thought by undermining the role of philosophical speculation. It is perhaps too much to claim that al-Ghazali renewed the Islamic religion, as it is sometimes suggested, but it is certainly the case that his influence was powerfully felt right through the Middle Ages and even into modern times.

Ibn Rushd

Ibn Rushd, also know by his Latinized name Averroes, spent most of his life fighting a rearguard battle against pressure to exclude philosophy from Islamic orthodoxy. He rejected the then common view that philosophical speculation over matters of religion is irreligious but argued rather that it is commanded by God.

Born: 1126, Córdoba, Spain
Importance: Insisted that philosophy was compatible with Islam
Died: 1198, Marrakesh, Morocco

Moreover, he denied that the conclusions of philosophers tended to run contrary to scripture, insisting that it had long been understood by Muslims that the Qur'an is open to more than one interpretation.

His defense of philosophical reason against its critics is probably best exemplified in his twelfth-century work *The Incoherence of Incoherence* (*Tuhafut al-Tuhafut*), a response to al-Ghazali's *The Incoherence of the Philosophers*. Al-Ghazali had aimed to show that the theories of philosophers such as Ibn Sina (Avicenna) were both incoherent in their own terms and also un-Islamic. For example, he attacked the view that the world was eternal on the grounds that the Qur'an is full of references to its creation, and that to the extent that God is an agent, it is perfectly reasonable to suppose that he was able to create the world *ex nihilo*, and then to destroy it again if he so chooses.

Ibn Rushd's critique of al-Ghazali's conception of divine agency is indicative of the kinds of methods that he employed. He argued that al-Ghazali made the mistake of assuming that God, like us, is a temporal agent. If we decide to do something, we can delay our action if we so choose, or embark upon it and then take a break before continuing. It doesn't work this way for God. He is present at all times; therefore, there is nothing to differentiate one time from another to allow him to delay an action.

Moreover, according to Ibn Rushd, there isn't anything that can function as a barrier to God's actions. His nature is perfect and unchanging; it doesn't make sense to suppose that he can wait for an appropriate moment before creating the world. Indeed, the whole idea of God having desires that are equivalent to human desires is incoherent. There is no possibility of the kind of change in God's nature that the fulfilment of desires entails.

Ibn Rushd's philosophical speculations on religious matters were not exclusively defensive. He also produced a number of arguments in favor of the existence of God, claiming that the fact that the Universe suits the purposes of human beings, and the fact that all living things are so clearly designed, is proof of God's reality. He also wrote influentially on non-religious matters. His translations of the works of Aristotle, and the accompanying commentaries, reintroduced Aristotle to the Western world, and are still admired. Even if his endeavors were ultimately unsuccessful, it is for his defense of philosophical reason, waged in the face of considerable opposition, that he is rightly celebrated.

Divine agency: Refers to God's ability to act, make choices, and perhaps most significantly to intervene in the world of his creation. Reflection on these issues quickly leads into complex arguments. For example, if God is perfectly good, to what extent is he constrained in his actions?

Ibn al-Arabi

Ibn al-Arabi, known as "The Great Master," represents perhaps the apex in Islamic mystical thought. However, his writings are far from easy to understand, and they are subject to a number of different interpretations. Partly this is because of the difficulties of translation from Arabic, but it is also because the ideas themselves are complex and somewhat alien to modern sensibilities.

Born: 1164, Murcia, Spain
Importance: The greatest of the Sufi mystical thinkers
Died: 1240, Damascus, Syria

Consider, for example, his beliefs about God. A central Islamic principle is that God is eternal, omniscient, and omnipotent. He is unchanging and undifferentiated. However, this notion leads to problems in conceptualizing God's relation to our everyday world. How is it possible for God to come to know about changes in the world without changing himself?

Ibn al-Arabi's answer is that the everyday world is in some way a part of God; it is an aspect of his essence or unity. Thus al-Arabi talks of a Oneness of Being (*wahdat al-wujud*), claiming that all apparent division, tension, and contradiction in the world is in fact a facet of a single reality. This idea has resulted in him being characterized as a pantheist (someone who believes that God is everything). However, Islamic scholars reject this view, arguing that his thought is more sophisticated than this characterization would suggest. The trouble is this sophistication makes al-Arabi's precise view very difficult to grasp. Here, for example, is his translator, R.W.J. Austin's attempt:

> What he says of the relationship between the Cosmos and God is that the Cosmos is not and cannot be other than God, not that it is God or that God is the Cosmos. His doctrine of

Left: Al-Arabi believed that God was omnipresent and that the everyday world was part of God; however, God is also separate from our world and therefore remains unaltered, even if the world itself changes.

the Oneness of Being . . . means that the sole, whole Reality is far more than the sum of its parts or aspects and that, however things may seem from the standpoint of differentiated being or perception, all being is nothing other than Its Being . . .

Not all his ideas are this opaque. For example, he talks about the various paths to true knowledge in terms that are fairly standard in the mystical tradition. He argues that there are three levels of knowledge, which are, roughly speaking, knowledge based on reason, empirical knowledge, and divine knowledge. The first two kinds of knowledge are subordinate to, and in a certain aspect are contained by, the third kind. However, al-Arabi did not believe that humans could actively gain divine knowledge. Rather, it would be revealed only to those primed to receive it.

An assessment of Ibn al-Arabi's importance is in one sense difficult because his work is still to be exhaustively studied. However, there is no doubting his influence. He is considered probably the greatest exponent of Sufi mysticism. For some, this status makes him an apostate whose teachings are to be resisted. For others, he is regarded as a visionary whose memory is to be honored.

Monotheism

Monotheism is the doctrine that there is only one God or that God is a unity. The God of monotheism is entirely separate from the rest of reality. In a sense, monotheism holds there are two fundamental realities: God and everything else.

The great monotheistic religions of the world, Judaism, Christianity, and Islam, are all committed to the idea of a creator God:

> In the beginning God created the heavens and the earth. Now the earth was formless and empty, darkness was over the surface of the deep, and the Spirit of God was hovering over the waters. (Genesis 1:1–2)

The God of monotheism does not simply create, and then disappear. He has an ongoing involvement in his creation, sustaining it through his divine will. He is a personal God who takes an interest in the lives of human beings. He is the source of the ethical framework by which they should live and has the power to grant all the people he created eternal life (or not).

Monotheism tends to be jealously guarded. Thus, for example, the Ten Commandments begin with an assertion of Yahweh's preeminence:

> And God spoke all these words:
> "I am the LORD your God, who brought you out of Egypt, out of the land of slavery.
> You shall have no other gods before me." (Exodus 20:1–3)

Although Yahweh here does not explicitly rule out the existence of lesser gods, he leaves the Israelites in no doubt that he alone is the real thing.

The religion that makes the most of its monotheism is Islam. One of the Five Pillars of Islam — in fact, the most important — holds that "there is none worthy of worship except Allah (God) and that Muhammad is His last messenger." This is subject to strict interpretation. Many Muslims consider Christianity to be a polytheistic religion (a religion of many gods) because it is committed to the notion of the Trinity (Father, Son, and Holy Spirit). For a Muslim, to be accused of polytheism is to be accused of the worst kind of apostasy. Indeed, according to the Wahhabis, dominant in Saudi Arabia, it is to forfeit the right to life and/or property.

There are a number of complexities associated with monotheism. Perhaps the most interesting concerns what is called "the problem of evil." This has to do with how to reconcile God's omnipotence, omniscience, and omnibenevolence (being all-good) with the existence of evil in the world. If God is the single creator of the world, where does evil come from? There is no entirely satisfactory answer to this question — it has troubled theologians for more than a thousand years — however, one response is to invoke the existence of an entity that has supernatural powers which are employed for nefarious purposes, for example, Ahriman in Zoroastrianism, and Satan in the Christian tradition. However, it is not clear that this will work as a solution to the problem of evil, while at the same time allowing a religion to remain properly monotheistic.

Ibn Taymiyya

Ibn Taymiyya's insistence on the literal interpretation of the Qur'an influenced many Muslims, both contemporary and future. He stood against anything that distorted what he took to be the original and true meaning of Islam, as set out and practiced by Muhammad, his contemporaries, and the first three generations of Muslims.

Born: 1263, Harran, Turkey
Importance: Criticized both philosophical and mystical texts for their departure from the proper tenets of Islam
Died: 1328, Damascus, Syria

Taymiyya was very clear about what he did not like: the Mongols, the Sufis, most religious shrines, the Shiites, metaphorical interpretations of the Qur'an. He argued that divine revelation is the only proper source of knowledge about God and His plans for the world. Human reason necessarily plays a secondary role to a proper understanding of the Qur'an and the lessons of the Sunnah (the words and deeds of Muhammad as set out in the hadith). This view led him to criticize Islamic thinkers such as Ibn Sina who used philosophical methods in order to examine religious questions. For example, Taymiyya insisted it is possible to know about the attributes of God without engaging in philosophical speculation. It was his view that God should be described "as he has described himself in his book and as the Prophet has described him in his Sunnah." It follows then that if the Qur'an says that God is seated on a throne, that is where he is seated.

Taymiyya's criticisms were not restricted to people who were inclined towards philosophy. He also had harsh words for those attracted to mysticism, and for Sufism, in general, which he felt represented a far more worrying trend than anything coming out of the work of the philosophers. His argument here was the obverse of his argument about philosophical reason. People who engage in mysticism are seduced by the power of strong emotion. They tend to assume that what they experience in emotional states is genuine and truthful, whereas in fact it is unreliable precisely because it is the product of emotion rather than revelation. His message here is again that it is only by the Qur'an and the Sunnah that people can come to know the truth about God and their responsibilities towards him.

Somewhat ironically, Taymiyya's Qur'anic literalism got him into trouble for heresy. He was accused of the sin of anthropomorphism; that is, of believing, for example, that the hand, foot, and face of God are literal, humanlike attributes. He was imprisoned several times for his unorthodox and provocative views, and eventually died in prison, it is said because he couldn't bear to be without his books.

> If the Qur'an attributes a throne to Allah . . . it is then known that this throne is, with respect to Allah, like the elevated seat is with respect to other than Allah. And this makes it necessarily true that He is on top of the throne.
>
> Taymiyya, *Maqalat*

Although Taymiyya's ideas were unpopular with the religious authorities of his day, he had a strong following among the general populace. He also bequeathed a significant legacy to the future. His ideas influenced Abd al-Wahhab, the great 18th century Muslim revivalist preacher, whose views in turn have been influential in the rise of modern Islamic fundamentalism.

Muhammad al-Wahhab

Muhammad al-Wahhab, the founder of the Wahhabi movement, believed that the Islam of his day had been corrupted by outside influences. His teachings were aimed at the purification of Islam. He sought to return the Muslim community to what he regarded as the original principles of Islam and to purge any changes introduced by innovation (*bida*).

Born: 1703, Uyaynah, Saudi Arabia

Importance: The founder of Wahhabism, the dominant form of Islam in Saudi Arabia

Died: 1792, Diriyah, Saudi Arabia

Al-Wahhab shared Taymiyya's literal interpretation of the Qu'ran, together with his condemnation of beliefs and practices that could be interpreted as polytheistic. For example, he eschewed the veneration of saints and prophets, arguing that pilgrimages to their graves were inappropriate, and he condemned the celebration of Muhammad's birthday.

Taymiyya's influence is also clear in al-Wahhab's views about Muslims who did not accept his strict interpretation of Islam. Al-Wahhab claimed that these Muslims were polytheists and therefore not believers of the true faith. Al-Wahhab's uncompromising attitude towards what he regarded as deviant religious practices led him to be particularly intolerant of Sufism, which he regarded as the source of many polytheistic practices.

It would not, however, be right to characterize al-Wahhab as a reactionary. Although he was strict about what constituted proper Islamic faith, there is also a sense in which he was an Islamic reformer. He insisted that Muslims should not blindly follow religious leaders, but rather interpret the Qur'an and the hadith for themselves. This injunction followed naturally from his belief that the fundamentals of Islam are to be found in the words and deeds of Muhammad.

Al-Wahhab's doctrine did not in its early stages attract many followers. This changed after he forged a pact with Muhammad Ibn Saud, an Arab chieftain. As a result, Wahhabism became important in the formation and development of the kingdom of Saudi Arabia. To this day, the country's Grand Muftis (the highest official of religious law in a Sunni Muslim country) are appointed from among al-Wahhab's descendants.

Wahhabism makes considerable demands on its adherents. In its modern form, it includes the following in the list of practices that are antithetical to Islam: photographing and drawing people; listening to music and watching television; wearing charms; celebrating the annual feasts of Sufi saints; practicing magic; and praying to anybody or anything other than God.

Jihad: A contested Islamic term that literally means "struggle," but which refers variously to an inner struggle for spiritual purity, the struggle to mobilize the Muslim community in the service of Islam, and a "holy war" fought to defend — or promulgate — Islam.

Wahhabism has come under increasing scrutiny in recent years, particularly with the rise of the Taliban in Afghanistan (who are said to be inspired by the doctrine, even though they are not themselves Wahhabists). Among Muslims, opinion is divided about al-Wahhab. He is considered by many to be a pious scholar, even if it is believed that his interpretation of Islam is overly proscriptive. For other Muslims, his ideas are just too radical. His own brother criticized his view that even Muslims who follow the five pillars of Islam may still be considered infidels if they do not adhere to strict Wahhabist doctrines.

The Philosopher-Poet

Muhammad Iqbal

Muhammad Iqbal, one of the great Islamic poets, is perhaps best known now for his politics. He was an enthusiastic supporter of the idea of a worldwide Islamic community, a New Mecca, in which all Muslims — in fact, all people — would be united, free of the divisions of race, nationality, and caste. Later in his career, despite his earlier opposition to the idea, he achieved both fame and notoriety by calling for an independent Muslim state to be established in northwestern India.

Born: 1877, Sialkot, India
Importance: The outstanding Muslim thinker of the twentieth century
Died: 1938, Lahore, India

Iqbal insisted that Islam by its very nature is a religion bound up with the social order. Therefore, it is not possible for a Muslim community to exist happily within a society that is not organized on Islamic principles. In particular, if the polity is secular then it will inevitably weaken the structures that bind Muslims to each other and their faith. A criticism that is sometimes leveled at Iqbal is that these kinds of ideas necessarily promote a deeply entrenched separatism. Iqbal, however, denied this, countering that

All men and not Muslims alone are meant for the Kingdom of God on Earth, provided they say goodbye to their idols of race and nationality and treat one another as personalities . . . my aim is simply to discover a universal social reconstruction.

Iqbal's advocacy of a specifically Islamic social and political order is puzzling, since his philosophical writings, at least at first, seem to be far removed from this sort of concern. Their central focus is the self, and the claim that the purpose of life is to develop and perfect the self through engagement with the will of

God. This was achieved to the greatest effect by the Prophet Muhammad, who provides a model for the rest of humanity.

Iqbal stressed that human beings actively have to seek their freedom and immortality. We enjoy an exalted status as "God's vicegerents," but with this comes the injunction to carry out his will. The committed Muslim must take on a responsibility for the world as directed in the Qur'an and seek to produce the ideal Islamic society. Personal fulfillment as an expression of freedom is absolutely bound up with an involvement in the wider Islamic community. It is this fact that brings politics to center stage.

> Politics have their roots in the spiritual life of Man. It is my belief that Islam is not a matter of private opinion. It is a society, or if you like, a civic Church. It is because present-day political ideals . . . may affect its original structure and character that I find myself interested in politics.
>
> *Thoughts and Reflections of Iqbal*

Although Iqbal did not live to see Pakistan established in 1947, he is remembered as being its spiritual father — in Pakistan they celebrate Iqbal Day. He has also retained his reputation as a poet and philosopher of the highest order. It is generally accepted that he is the outstanding Muslim thinker of the twentieth century.

Sayyid Qutb

Sayyid Qutb is perhaps the most influential of the twentieth century's radical Muslim thinkers. The Islamic fundamentalism he preached, though extremely contentious and indeed widely rejected within the Muslim world, has been used to justify the use of violence in the name of Islam. Indeed, many people believe Qutb's ideas have played a key part in the emergence of Al-Qaeda.

Born: 1906, Musha, Egypt
Importance: Sought the reestablishment of an Islamic caliphate, if necessary through the use of violence
Died: 1966, Cairo, Egypt

Writing in the middle of the twentieth century, Qutb claimed that mankind had reached a moment of crisis. A secular worldview had caused people to see God and religion as divorced from everyday life. It was Qutb's fear that this secular outlook, already running unchecked in the West, would come to dominate the Muslim world. He was, for example, deeply worried by Kemal Ataturk's rule in Turkey, which had seen the forward march of secular ideas in a onetime Muslim state.

According to Qutb, Islam is more than a faith but in fact an all-encompassing system of law, governance, and morality. However, piecemeal and partial application of Sharia law had caused the Muslim world to revert to a pre-Islamic state of godless ignorance (*jahiliyya*). This situation could only be reversed by establishing a vanguard of true Muslims, who would aim to resurrect the caliphate and establish a society based on Sharia law. Qutb argued that this vanguard movement must separate itself from the corrupting influence of contemporary society. It is only through the mechanism of separation by migration (*hijra*) that an Islamic community, true to Islamic law, could be established.

Left: Qutb believed that Muslims should separate from an increasingly secular society in order to remain pure and true to Allah.

Qutb argued that a Muslim vanguard should fight against *jahiliyya* in two ways. Firstly, by the simple mechanism of preaching the truth of Islam. Secondly, and more controversially, by "physical power and jihad." He did not think that the move to restore an authentic Islamic community would be easy. Rather, he talked of struggle, sacrifice, and martyrdom. He praised those Muslims who were willing to sacrifice themselves for Islam, claiming that believers "who risk their lives and go out to fight, and who are prepared to lay down their lives for the cause of God are honorable people, pure of heart, and blessed of soul."

Qutb did not believe that a society based on Sharia law would be primitive or brutal. It is, of course, true that Sharia sanctions punishments that in the West are thought to be brutal, such as amputation for theft. However, in contrast to non-Sharia societies, which force people to worship their human rulers, a society organized along Islamic precepts requires only that man submit to the divine rule of God.

Unsurprisingly, Qutb's views have been criticized by Islamic and Western scholars alike. Mainstream Muslims reject the idea that "physical power and jihad" can ever legitimately be used to destroy the institutions of *jahiliyya*.

Ayatollah Khomeini

One of the greatest turning points of the twentieth century occurred in February 1979, when Ayatollah Khomeini, an elderly Shi'ite cleric, returned to Iran after fifteen years in exile to establish the country as an Islamic republic.

Born: 1902, Khomein, Iran
Importance: Supreme Leader of the Islamic revolution in Iran
Died: 1989, Tehran, Iran

The events that unfolded in Iran that year surprised the world, but in fact Khomeini's blueprint for Islamic government had been set out in a series of lectures that were published in 1971 as *Velayat-e Faqih: Hokumat-e Islami* (*Islamic Government Under the Guardianship of the Jurist*). In these lectures, he argued that Iran should not be a monarchy but an Islamic republic. The republic would be ruled by an Islamic jurist (*faqih*), to be chosen by the clergy, and its laws would be based on Sharia law.

Khomeini's ideas on Islamic government were revolutionary. The orthodox view of Shiite Muslims had been that until the Hidden Imam returned to Earth to establish a reign of divine justice, the responsibility for political affairs would lie with a largely secular state (though in some versions of this doctrine there would a greater or lesser role for Islamic jurists).

Khomeini rejected this view, arguing that God would not have given mankind the Qur'an and the explicit rules for living that it contains if it had not been intended that it should be implemented. Moreover, he argued that it was clear that both Muhammad and Imam Ali had intended that Sharia law should be enforced by the most learned jurists until the return of the Hidden Imam. The need to establish an Islamic state was pressing because, left to their own devices, human beings were not going to lead good Muslim lives.

In political terms, Khomeini was spectacularly successful in the short term. The Constitution of Iran, which affords the country's Supreme Leader almost unlimited powers, was implemented in December 1979 following a popular referendum. Sharia law was introduced under Khomeini and rigorously enforced in the early years following the revolution.

However, Khomeini's ideas have not been universally embraced even within Shiite society. For example, Grand Ayatollah Kho'i, one of Khomeini's fiercest critics, identified two principled reasons for opposing the theory of *velayat-e faqih*. Firstly, he argued that the authority of the *fuqaha* — Islamic jurists who determine how Sharia is to be interpreted and applied in particular circumstances — could not be extended by merely human decree to the political sphere. Secondly, he denied that the authority of Islamic jurists should be restricted to just one or a few of them.

> Man is half angel, half devil. The devil part is always stronger than the angel part. This is why society should organize to combat it through laws and suitable punishments.
>
> Khomeini, *Explication of Issues*

It is too early to judge the lasting influence of Khomeini's ideas about Islamic government. However, it is certainly not possible to understand the political landscape of the present day without an appreciation of his role in establishing Iran as the world's first Islamic state.

Jewish Movements

Judaism is a religion of movements and tendencies that interact in a number of complex ways. The situation is one of engagement, rather than schism, thus distinguishing Judaism from the other Abrahamic religions, Christianity and Islam. A further distinction here is that Judaism is characterized by a number of ethnic divisions, particularly between the Ashkenazi, Sephardic, and Mizrahi communities.

Perhaps the best starting point to get a sense of Judaism's various movements is to consider the impact of the eighteenth-century Enlightenment — which emphasized the power of rational thought, universal values, and scientific progress — on Ashkenazi, or more broadly, European Jews. There was, in fact, a specific Jewish Enlightenment, or Haskalah movement, which aimed at increasing Jewish integration into European secular society. In particular, Jews were urged to adopt the rationalism of the Enlightenment, to study secular subjects, and to learn European as well as Hebrew languages.

Its religious analog was the Jewish Reform movement which emerged in Germany in the early nineteenth century, and continues to this day in various forms. Early Reform Judaism denied that the Torah was divinely authored, rejected much of traditional Jewish law, replaced the Hebrew prayer book with a German version, abandoned the practice of Kashrut, and abolished circumcision. Although Reform Judaism originated in Germany, its great success occurred when it was imported into the United States in the 1840s, where even today it is the largest Jewish grouping, though in a modified form.

Perhaps the movement that contrasts most obviously with Reform Judaism is Orthodox Judaism. Indeed, the term "orthodox" was first used by Reformers to label their traditionalist adversaries. In the present day, Orthodox Judaism, which is dominant in Israel, holds that the Torah and Talmud are inerrant, and therefore that they alone form the proper basis for religious observance. In practice, among other things, this means strict observance of the Sabbath and religious festivals, daily worship, Kashrut, prayers and ceremonies in their traditional form, and the separation of men and women in the synagogue.

Orthodox Judaism, though, is by no means uniform. There are differences, for example, in the extent of engagement with secular society, the importance assigned to the study of the Torah and the scope of its application, the respective roles of men and women, and so on. Moreover, the extent to which those people who formally adhere to Orthodoxy follow its strictures varies enormously. In the United Kingdom, for example, the evidence is that the mass of its members is less religiously inclined than the official position might suggest.

Reform and Orthodox Judaism are by no means the only Jewish movements or tendencies. Others include Conservative or Masorti Judaism, Reconstructionist Judaism, Hasidism, Jewish Renewal, and Humanistic Judaism. These vary in the liberalism of their theological positions and in the strictness of their interpretation of Jewish law. It would be a mistake, however, to suppose that a liberal theological position necessarily means a relaxed approach to Jewish law. The Jewish faith is complex — as is evidenced by the subtle distinctions between and within its various movements and tendencies — which makes this an open question.

Moses

Moses is arguably the most important figure in the history of - Judaism. He was born at a time when the Hebrew people were living under the yoke of Egyptian rule. According to tradition, some eighty years into his life, he encountered God (*Yahweh* in Hebrew) in a burning bush, and was commanded to free the Hebrews from their slavery. This he achieved, after Egypt had suffered a number of plagues at the hands of Yahweh, and the Red Sea had parted, allowing Moses, together with the Hebrews, to pass through.

Born: Ca. fourteenth century
BCE, Egypt
Importance: The most
significant prophet and
leader of the Jews
Died: Ca. thirteenth century
BCE, Moab, Jordan

Their immediate destination was the Sinai Peninsula. It was here that Moses ascended Mount Sinai, where it is said that he spent forty days and nights with Yahweh, before descending with two tablets, on which were inscribed the ten commandments that represented a covenant between Yahweh and the Hebrews, the Decalogue.

The covenant was predicated upon the indebtedness of the Hebrews to the God who had favored them. Yahweh had delivered the Jews from the tyranny of Egyptian rule; the Hebrews in their turn were to pledge allegiance to him. Thus, the Decalogue begins with an assertion of Yahweh's absolute preeminence:

You shall have no other gods before me.

To the modern Western mind, there is nothing particularly striking about these words. Yet at a time where polytheism was the norm, they were, in effect, a declaration of monotheism, establishing Judaism as a religion of just one God. This was

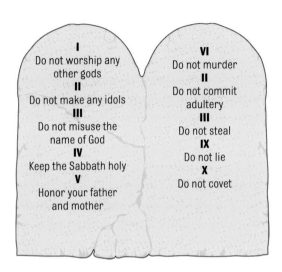

I
Do not worship any
other gods

II
Do not make any idols

III
Do not misuse the
name of God

IV
Keep the Sabbath holy

V
Honor your father
and mother

VI
Do not murder

II
Do not commit
adultery

III
Do not steal

IX
Do not lie

X
Do not covet

Above: Moses received the Decalogue, or the Ten Commandments, from God.

reaffirmed in the injunctions that prohibited the Israelites from creating representations of Yahweh or taking his name in vain.

The Decalogue also contains a number of commands that are suitable for the purpose of building a stable and secure community. Moses was aware that unless these rules were backed up by a system of expiation then they would not function properly. Thus, he constructed a Tabernacle and established a priesthood, whose members were able to conduct rituals of atonement, thereby establishing the basis for the emergence of the Hebrew religion proper.

The importance of Moses in the Jewish faith cannot be overstated. Indeed, according to Jewish tradition, he was the author of the Pentateuch, which was dictated to him directly by God. Though it is now believed that the Pentateuch was the work of more than one author, Moses is still seen as the person who brought the Torah to Israel and therefore as the primary intercessor between God and the Hebrews.

Hillel the Elder

Hillel the Elder, a Jewish sage and contemporary of King Herod, was responsible for establishing precise rules for the analysis of Scripture — the Seven Rules of Hillel, which were influential for many centuries.

Born: Ca. 60 BCE, Babylon
Importance: Established precise rules for the analysis of Scripture
Died: Ca. 10 CE, Jerusalem

Hillel is remembered as a man of peace, a friend to all men, a committed and diligent teacher, a passionate scholar of Jewish Scripture, and a man of great patience and restraint. Although it is possible that history has exaggerated his personal qualities, we do know that Hillel valued in other people, and in Judaism more generally, precisely those characteristics that he is said to have exhibited.

Hillel considered brotherly love to be the core truth of the Jewish religion. This "Golden Rule," which exhorts man to treat others as he would like to be treated himself, is found in most of the major religions and in modern thinking about ethics.

Hillel's religious sensibility was not, however, exhausted in the injunction to love one's fellow man. He was also a ferocious advocate of the importance of the study of scripture and the law. One account records that he stood in Jerusalem one day accosting people as they went to work, asking them how much they earned. When they replied, he suggested that they would be better off studying the Torah, since in this way

> That which is hateful to you, do not do to your neighbor. That is the whole Torah; the rest is commentary, the explanation; go and study it.

they would possess all that they would need for this world and the next.

Although he was passionate about the Torah, he did not restrict its interpretation. In contrast to his contemporary and rival Shammai, Hillel advocated a liberal interpretation. This enabled him to tailor his rulings to the socioeconomic conditions of the times. For example, despite a contrary extant law rooted in Biblical exegesis, he enacted the *Prozbul*, a legal injunction that ensured that creditors received repayment of their loans, removing the fear that by lending money to the poor it might be lost.

The different exegetical principles employed by Hillel and Shammai were sustained after their deaths by their disciples in the Beit Hillel (the House of Hillel) and the Beit Shammai (the House of Shammai). The Talmud records over 300 differences of opinion between the two houses. With very few exceptions, the views of the House of Hillel were established as the legal norm.

Hillel's influence on Jewish life was profound. The leaders of the Jews in Palestine until the fifth century were his descendents, and today some of the most popular stories in Jewish folklore concern Hillel, particularly his dealings with his rival Shammai.

Judaism

Philo of Alexandria

According to Philo of Alexandria, the goal of a human life is to come to knowledge of "the true and living God, who is the first and most perfect of all good things; from whom, as from a fountain, all particular blessings are showered upon the world, and upon the things and people in it."

Born: 15–10 BCE, Alexandria
Importance: The foremost exponent of Hellenistic Judaism
Died: 45–50 CE, Alexandria

In Philo's philosophy, however, the task of knowing God is far from straightforward. The problem is that while it is possible to know that God exists by reflecting on the natural world and our powers of reason, the knowledge of his essence lies beyond the capabilities of human beings. He maintains that God is wholly transcendent. He exists neither in time nor space. He has no attributes and consequently is beyond our perception. He is unchangeable, eternal, and immutable. Philo referenced God's own words to Moses in Exodus 3:14, to communicate a sense of this idea: "I am who I am."

Although Philo believed God to be in one sense utterly separate from humanity and the world, he also thought, somewhat paradoxically, that God is connected to the world, both as its creator and maintainer. To square this apparent circle, he employed a notion he termed the "Logos." It isn't clear precisely what this notion entails. Many commentators on Philo's work suggest that he wasn't consistent in the way he used the concept. Perhaps the best way to think of it is just as that aspect of Divinity — both immanent in the world, yet transcendent of it — that is accessible to human thought.

There is an element of mysticism in Philo's treatment of the precise mechanisms whereby human beings come into contact with the Logos He talked about a "sober intoxication" which is characteristic of the state of being a person inhabits when she has left the material realm behind to enter into the eternal realm. Indeed, Philo suggested that it is possible in such a state to gain a direct apprehension of God as simply being One.

This idea that an apprehension of God is possible if the material world is cast off is indicative of the general suspicion with which Philo treated earthly existence. Drawing from stoicism, his idea of the perfectly ethical life involved conquering passion and living a life according to wisdom steeped in the exercise of reason. He considered the consequence of ethical failure to be a loss of the power of rational judgment as one becomes a slave to one's passions, driven by desires that are never satisfied. Virtue, in contrast, involves dispassionateness and moderation, which are dependent upon divine wisdom.

The influence of Philo of Alexandria's work has not been overwhelming. His idea of the Logos had some on impact the development of Christian theology. However, his work was unknown to medieval Jewish philosophers, and wasn't rediscovered until the sixteenth century. Perhaps the lasting interest of Philo's ideas is that they are exemplary in showing how it is possible to fuse the concepts of Greek philosophy with the themes of the Judaic religion.

Stoicism: A school of philosophy originating in ancient Greece that emphasized the importance of rationality and restraint in the face of the emotions, desires, and troubles that confront people in their everyday lives. Stoics emphasized four primary virtues: wisdom, justice, courage, and temperance.

The Historian

Josephus

The works of Josephus are some of the most comprehensive histories that we have of the Greco-Roman period. They offer an invaluable insight into both the history of Judaism in this era and the development of early Christianity.

Born: Ca. 37 CE, Jerusalem
Importance: One of the most important historians of the Greco-Roman period
Died: Ca. 100 CE, probably in Rome

In order to understand the significance of Josephus's works, it is necessary to know a little bit about the circumstances in which they were written. Josephus, born Joseph ben Mattathias in Jerusalem, during a time of Roman occupation, served as the commander of the Jewish forces in Galilee during the Great Revolt against Rome in 66–73 CE. When the Romans triumphed he was brought before their leader Vespasian, where he pulled a neat trick. He foretold that Vespasian would become a great Emperor, a conceit that saved his life. Two years later, when Vespasian did become Emperor of Rome, Josephus was released, given Roman citizenship, and he entered the patronage of the Emperor.

These circumstances mean that his reputation is mixed. His great work, *The Jewish War* (75–79 CE), for example, benefited from the access that he had to Rome's historical records. However, many people question its neutrality. Though Josephus showed some compassion for the suffering of the innocent Jews of Jerusalem, he nevertheless claimed that responsibility for the bloodshed of the Jewish–Roman War lay primarily with Jewish fanatics, such as the Zealots, rather than with the Romans.

Nevertheless, throughout his life Josephus remained interested in the situation and welfare of the Jews. In *Against the Greeks* (93 CE), for example, he defended Judaism, arguing that its customs compared favorably to those of the Greeks. And in

Jewish Antiquities (93 CE) he attempted to explain the history, law, and customs of the Jews to a non-Jewish audience. One of the most significant features of this work is that it contains the only first-century reference to the existence of Jesus by a non-Christian writer.

This passage is recorded in *Antiquities of the Jews* xviii 3.3:

> Now there was about this time Jesus, a wise man, if it be lawful to call him a man . . . He was Christ. And when Pilate, at the suggestion of the principal men amongst us, had condemned him to the cross, those that loved him at the first did not forsake him; for he appeared to them alive again the third day; as the divine prophets had foretold these and ten thousand other wonderful things concerning him. And the tribe of Christians, so named from him, are not extinct at this day.

Jewish attitudes to Josephus vary considerably. His critics consider him to be a traitor to the Jewish cause for his cooperation with the Roman invaders. They question his reliability as a historian and view his works as Roman propaganda or a self-serving defense of his own actions in the Jewish–Roman War. Others defend Josephus, arguing that in the Roman world of his day, the only realistic way of going forward was to engage in his kind of apologetics. It is unlikely that there will ever be a consensus about his proper reputation, but what is certain is that Josephus produced some of the most interesting and important works of history of this period.

Scripture

Scripture is the collective term to describe the holy texts of the religions of the world. Examples of scripture include the Jewish Torah, the New Testament of Christianity, the Islamic Qur'an, the Hindu Sruti, and the Analects of Confucianism.

These texts all have in common that they are considered to be sacred by the devotees of the religions of which they are part. Indeed, among the devout, scripture is often believed to contain the revealed world of God. Thus, for example, according to Jewish tradition, Yahweh dictated the Torah directly to Moses, who simply recorded what he was told. Similarly, Muslims believe that the Qur'an is the inspired word of Allah relayed to the Prophet Muhammad by the Angel Gabriel.

There is an interesting contrast between these two cases which tells us something about the various attitudes that it is possible to have towards scripture. The number of Jewish people who still believe that the Torah is the work of Moses alone is not great. Indeed, it is possible to find Jewish theologians who will deny that the Torah is the sacred word of God at all. There is no equivalent of this in the Muslim world. It is Islamic orthodoxy that the Qur'an is self-authenticating, precisely because it is the world of Allah as it was communicated to Muhammad. According to Muslim theologians, there is no such thing as Islamic fundamentalism because all Muslims accept that the Qur'an comprises the true word of Allah (though there is argument about what this is and how it is to be identified).

Perhaps the most interesting example of the authority of a sacred text is that of the Guru Granth Sahib, the holy book of Sikh religion. First compiled by Guru Arjan Dev, the fifth of the Sikh Gurus, it comprises the religion's sacred hymns and words. It was put together in its final form by Guru Gobind Singh, the tenth and final Guru, who declared that it, rather than another person, would be his successor. Thus, Sikhs treat the Guru Granth Sahib as if it were a living Guru. Sikhism then is a religion without a priestly hierarchy. The Granth (holy book) is available for everybody to read within Sikh temples, exemplifying and reaffirming the Sikh commitment to the equality and the universality of their religion.

It is not the case, however, that religious devotion requires a commitment to the truth of specific sacred texts. There is, for example, a non-realist strand in Christian thought that holds that God has a symbolic existence (or cultural significance), but that's it. This requires that the Bible is read metaphorically, not as if it were the repository of literal truths. And it is also possible for scripture to be sacred, and yet for there to be no claim that it is divinely inspired. This is the case with the sacred books of Taoism and Confucianism, which were written by men for men, and were originally viewed as such. However, though not the revealed word of God, they have over time achieved a sacrosanct status, and are every much as revered as the scripture of other religions.

Judaism

Moses Maimonides

Moses Maimonides, the greatest Jewish philosopher of the medieval era, would have had no sympathy with the Biblical literalism that is common today.He recognized, of course, that many of the stories of the Bible seem to have an obvious and straightforward meaning. However, the reality, he argued, is that religious truth is often hard to discern.

Born: 1135, Córdoba, Spain.
Importance: The leading intellectual of medieval Judaism.
Died: 1204, Egypt.

Consider, for example, the tendency of the Bible to anthropomorphize the characteristics of God. Maimonides denied that this is supposed to be taken literally. For example, although there are instances in the Bible where God is seen, these do not involve visual sightings, but rather intellectual accomplishments. Similarly, if the Bible talks about a prophet hearing God, this does not indicate an auditory phenomenon, but a prophet coming to an understanding of God's desires.

The suggestion that the Bible contains truths that are not immediately obvious raises the question of how one is supposed to identify them. The answer Maimonides gave in his great work *The Guide of the Perplexed* (late twelfth century) is that the revealed will of God will always be in harmony with reason. If there is a conflict between what reason teaches us and what the Bible seems to say, it is necessary to revisit the Bible in order to determine how we have misunderstood it. Thus, Maimonides claimed that if he had come to the conclusion that the Aristotelian view that matter is eternal was correct, then he would have had no difficulty in adjusting his view of the Biblical treatment of creation.

The Guide of the Perplexed is a difficult work; deliberately obscure, in fact, since Maimonides did not want to lead people into questioning their beliefs unless they were sophisticated enough to understand the answers that he was proposing. However, not all of his work is so difficult. He wrote, for example, a series of essays dealing with some of the philosophical issues raised by the rabbinic discussions of the Mishna. One of these essays presents the teachings of Judaism in Thirteen Articles of Faith. These are that a perfect, creator God exists; that he is a unity; that he is incorporeal; that he is eternal; that he communicates through prophecy; that the prophecy of Moses has priority; that God exclusively is to be worshipped; that the Torah had a divine origin; that the Torah is immutable; that there is divine providence; that there is divine reward and retribution; that there will be a Messiah; and that the dead will be resurrected. Maimonides's suggestion that there is such a thing as a Jewish dogma — a set of laws with binding force — sparked a controversy that hasn't been settled to this day.

Maimonides is a sophisticated thinker. Consequently, much of his thought requires a certain technical competence to be properly appreciated. But he is a thinker of considerable repute. His philosophical writings retain their interest for a contemporary audience, and within the Jewish tradition he has been proclaimed the "second Moses."

The Torah: The most important document in Judaism, the Torah comprises the first five books of the Tanakh: Genesis, Exodus, Leviticus, Numbers, and Deuteronomy, written out in Hebrew. The word "Torah" means "teaching" or "instruction," and the text is considered to be the primary guide to the Jewish faith.

Rashi

Rashi, whose name is an acronym for Rabbi Shlomo Yitzchaki, was the author of commentaries on the Talmud and the Tanakh, which arguably are unsurpassed in their importance and remain influential.

Born: 1040, Troyes, France
Importance: Produced
commentaries on the
Tanakh and the Talmud that
remain influential to this day
Died: 1105, Troyes, France

He was born in Troyes, France, in 1040, and lived the life of a scholar and teacher. It was an uneventful life, though he did survive the First Crusade which accounted for the deaths of 12,000 people in Lorraine. However, though his activities were low-key, his scholarly achievements were stunning.

The method he employed to analyze scripture rested on stating the meaning of a text as clearly and concisely as possible. He took pains to explain in simple terms any words that he thought were unclear. Moreover, he often illustrated the meaning of a text by using analogies from everyday life. For example, he might draw on a common experience of food or drink in order to make things clear. In addition, he would often employ existing rabbinical stories to clarify a text, assuming that his students would already be familiar with their meaning.

As an example, here is Rashi's commentary on Exodus 1:1.

Now these are the names of the sons of Israel who went into Egypt with Jacob, each with his family. . . . Though Scripture has previously enumerated them during their lifetime by their names, it again enumerates them at their deaths. This is to show how dear they are to God, because they are compared to the stars . . .

Rashi's work on the Talmud, in particular, was revolutionary in making the dense passages accessible to ordinary Jews. His treatment was detailed in a way that previous commentaries had not been. He used neither omission nor paraphrase to make is task easier, but rather dealt with the text, phrase by phrase, in its entirely.

Rashi's commentaries on both the Tanakh and the Talmud have become almost inseparable from the texts themselves. Nearly every printed version of these holy books contains his commentaries, and these have been accepted by Ashkenazi and Sephardi Jews alike. During the two centuries following Rashi's death, many French and German Talmud scholars devoted their lives to analyzing and elaborating upon his work. It would be hard to overestimate Rashi's significance in the Jewish world. Almost all Rabbinic literature published since his death engages with his work, either arguing against it or using it to support an author's own views.

Rashi's importance extends beyond the Jewish world. His work was influential in the development of Christian exegesis. In particular, Nicholas de Lyra, a noted Franciscan teacher and practitioner of Biblical exegesis, was strongly influenced by Rashi's commentaries. Martin Luther drew heavily on the work of de Lyra when he translated the Vulgate (the Latin translation of Bible) into German, and he incorporated some of Rashi's interpretations of text within his translation.

Talmud: A discussion of Jewish law, ethics, and history. The first part, the Mishnah, is a written compendium of Judaism's oral law. The second part, the Gemara, offers further analysis of the Mishnah as well as of the Tanakh.

Tanakh: The Hebrew bible, made up of the Torah, Nevi'im, and Ketuvim. It consists of twenty-four books.

Judaism

The Hasidic Jew

Baal Shem Tov

Rabbi Israel ben Eliezer, or Baal Shem Tov, as he is better known, the founder of Hasidic Judaism, was committed to a panentheistic view of God. He believed that God was immanent in the universe; or to put this another way, that God was contained in everything.

Born: 1698, Okop, Ukraine
Importance: The founder of
Hasidic Judaism
Died: 1760, Miedzyboz,
Ukraine

A number of things followed from this belief. First, since all things encompass a manifestation of God, it follows that something good must reside in everything. Therefore, in contrast to Christian orthodoxy, for example, Baal Shem Tov taught that humans were inherently good. It follows then that rather than condemning people for their sins, as if these are reflections of a thoroughly debased nature, one should attempt to explain them and to show how they are caused by folly rather than indwelling evil. Thus, Baal Shem Tov argued that no one was beyond redemption.

The idea that God is immanent in every person had other consequences. For example, it was common in the middle of the eighteenth century for orthodox Jews to mortify themselves through physical deprivation — perhaps by fasting. Baal Shem Tov, however, was opposed to asceticism and self-mortification. He considered care of the body important: if God is immanent in the body, it follows that the body cannot be considered to be somehow antagonistic to the divine.

You said that you must fast. I am deeply upset at your words. . . . You should not place yourself in this danger. This is the way of melancholy and sadness.

letter to Yaakov Yosef

90 91

Baal Shem Tov's panentheism also led him to claim that individuals have a duty to live out their lives in a spirit of holiness. Since all worldly acts are a manifestation of God, it follows that man must live in the light of this knowledge. His teachings were a critique of the Judaism practiced at the time. In the eighteenth century, many European Jews, subject to persecution, had taken refuge in academic study of the Talmud at the expense of their inner, spiritual lives. Baal Shem Tov argued that this practice was a misunderstanding of the nature of religious devotion, which requires an appreciation of spirituality and an awareness of the love of God.

Hasidic Judaism: A group that originated in Eastern Europe in the eighteenth century that concentrated on the spirituality and joy of the Jewish religion to counterbalance an academic emphasis at the time.

Significantly, the teachings of Baal Shem Tov were accessible even to the least educated of Jews. He taught that it was possible to attain great spirituality simply by loving God, other Jews, and spending time in the attitude of prayer. Indeed, he saw prayer as a state of consciousness where man becomes one with God. In the contemplation of the divine, God's immanence fills a person's heart with religious ecstasy.

Baal Shem Tov's teachings are not considered to be strikingly original, yet they transformed the Jewish world. He created a new religious atmosphere characterized by ritual, joy, and ecstasy. Hasidic Judaism has become a large movement which continues to be a force in the Jewish world to this day.

Moses Mendelssohn

The German Jewish philosopher, Moses Mendelssohn, is best known for his defences of Judaism. His arguments in favor of religious freedom, in conjunction with a commitment to the Enlightenment ideal of liberty, greatly furthered the cause of the emancipation of the German Jews.

Born: 1729, Dessau, Germany

Importance: Championed the cause of the Enlightenment and the emancipation of German Jews

Died: 1786, Berlin, Germany

Mendelssohn achieved fame almost by mistake. His friend Gotthold Lessing, the Enlightenment dramatist and philosopher, took it upon himself to publish Mendelssohn's *Philosophical Conversations* (1755) without first informing the author. The result was fame for Mendelssohn and the beginning of a career as a philosophical essayist. He is best known for his defences of Judaism, which were motivated by a critical article by theologian John Lavater. Lavater challenged Mendelssohn to become a Christian if he were not able to demonstrate the superiority of Judaism. Mendelssohn responded by dedicating his life to the cause of the Enlightenment and the emancipation of the German Jews.

To this end, he set about translating the Pentateuch and other parts of the Bible into German. His intention was to make it possible for Jews to participate fully in German culture. His translation was immediately popular, contributing to the emergence of the Haskalah movement, which aimed at increasing Jewish integration into European secular society. Particularly, Jews were urged to adopt the rationalism of the Enlightenment, to study secular subjects, and to learn European as well as Hebrew languages.

Mendelssohn's most important work, *Jerusalem* (1783), was a powerful argument for religious freedom. In it, he sought to demonstrate that the state has no right to interfere with the religious convictions of its citizens. Indeed, as far as convictions are concerned, the state is in exactly the same position as the church: "Both must teach, instruct, encourage, motivate." This is not, however, the case for behavioral control. Here the state enjoys a monopoly of coercive power. The complexity of civil society means that it will never be possible to govern simply by appealing to right convictions. Therefore, the state has

> The state has *physical power* and uses it when necessary; the power of religion is love and *beneficence*.

recourse to a system of reward and punishment in order to secure appropriate behavior. This is not available to a religion.

Mendelssohn's commitment to religious freedom was in large part motivated by his desire to see Jewish people everywhere free of economic, social, and political restriction. However, it also tied in with an Enlightenment commitment to liberty and freedom. It was Mendelssohn's view that in order to attain moral and intellectual perfection, individuals needed to be free to make mistakes, pursue their own goals, and to develop their own beliefs. However, despite his obvious liberalism, he remained committed to the distinctiveness and value of Judaic revelation to the extent that it laid down laws for living a certain kind of life.

Mendelssohn strove to strike a balance in his work between a commitment to Judaism and an accommodation of rationality and modern Western culture. Not every Jewish scholar agrees that he got the balance right. However, it is generally accepted that through his championing of religious tolerance, and through his own intellectual brilliance, he successfully furthered the cause of the emancipation of the German Jews.

Mordecai Kaplan

Mordecai Kaplan's Judaism is an unusual kind. He denied the existence of a supernatural God who is able to interfere in the affairs of the world. He rejected the idea that the Jewish people had been "chosen" for a specific purpose. He also denied that the established rituals and practices of the Jewish faith were inviolate, asserting, "the past has a vote, but not a veto."

Born: 1881, Svencionys, Lithuania

Importance: The founder of the twentieth century Reconstructionist movement in Judaism

Died: 1983, New York, United States

He was led to these views by what he saw as a crisis in Judaism. He argued that the rise in Naturalism had rendered a certain kind of religious belief untenable. In particular, it was no longer possible for Jewish people to accept the truth of their traditional theology. It was necessary, then, to consign to the past beliefs such as that God is a supernatural being, that the Torah is the divinely inspired word of God, that God intervenes in the natural world, and that people will be rewarded or punished in the afterlife depending on their behavior.

However, Kaplan did not believe that this meant that it was necessary to give up Judaism altogether. Rather, the aim must be to reconstruct the Jewish religion so that it properly reflects modern Jewish civilization. If this were achieved, then Judaism would function to bind the Jewish community together, enhancing Jewish identity.

His argument was inspired by the French sociologist Emile Durkheim, who believed that religion both reflected and reinforced the collective identity of the social group within which it was rooted. Thus, Kaplan subverted traditional Judaism by putting the Jewish community at the center of his theology rather than God.

These thoughts raise the question of the nature of a religion without supernatural elements. Did Kaplan envisage, for example, that his Judaism would retain a conception of God? He did, but his understanding of God was very different to the traditional God of the Torah. He argued that God is the power in the Universe that enables righteousness and facilitates human self-fulfillment.

Kaplan employed a similar strategy of reconceptualization when dealing with other traditional Judaic concepts. For example, he argued that divine revelation involved identifying those aspects of traditional belief that reflected universal human qualities, then integrating these into our modern belief systems, which would enable that part of the tradition that has no modern relevance simply to be abandoned.

Mordecai Kaplan's ideas formed the basis of the Jewish Reconstructionist movement that emerged in the second half of the twentieth century. However, they have attracted strong criticism. While many Jewish scholars accept that he has accurately described some of the problems facing the Jewish religion in the modern age, they often also believe that his reconstruction of Jewish theology is a step too far toward atheism. There is no doubting the radicalism of Kaplan's position. The issue is simply whether his ideas constitute a properly Judaic religious philosophy.

> To believe in God means to take for granted that it is man's destiny to rise above the brute and to eliminate all forms of violence and exploitation from human society.

Martin Buber

Martin (Mordechai) Buber, the existentialist Jewish philosopher and theologian, is best known for his religious philosophy of existence, introduced in his famous 1923 treatise *Ich und Du* (later translated into English as *I and Thou*). In this work, Buber used the word pairs "I–Thou" and "I–It" as a heuristic device to contrast different modes of being and relations to other people and things.

Born: 1878, Vienna, Austria
Importance: Showed how it was possible to marry existentialist themes with a religious worldview
Died: 1965, Jerusalem, Israel

The I–Thou constitutes a mutual, open, and authentic relation between two beings. It represents a definite encounter between one being and another in which there is no manipulation or objectification. The I–Thou then is pure, contentless, mutuality, as, for example, might exist between two lovers, or between a mother and her child. The concept can be used appropriately to describe the relation of one person to another, and also the relation of a person to an animal, to a plant, and even to God, the great Thou.

According to Buber, the I–Thou relationship is the only one that can exist between a person and God. It is not possible to talk truly about God or to describe him properly, but it is possible to *encounter* him in a revelation of the divine. Buber argued that all I–Thou relationships are ultimately connected to an interaction with God.

The I–It relation is almost the diametric opposite of the I–Thou. Buber characterized it as a confrontation with an object, rather than an encounter with a fellow being. There is no mutuality, no equality, and no genuine encounter in the I–It relation. Rather, a person relates to the other being in an objective, detached manner, seeing them in terms of how they

Above: The relationship a scientist has with the world is one of detachment: the I–It. In direct contrast is the I–Thou, such as the pure and mutual relationship between a mother and her child. This is the relationship between man and God.

might be of use. This kind of relation is exemplified by the scientist who examines data about the world. For Buber, the objects of these kinds of relations exist only as mental representations in the mind. Thus, the I–It relation is a monologue with oneself rather than an encounter or dialogue with another being.

Buber claimed that individuals always engage with the world in either I–Thou or I–It terms. He declared "All actual life is encounter." However, he thought the I–Thou encounter to be rare and was critical of what he saw as an increase in the I–It mode of relation between human beings, arguing that it rendered human existence less meaningful. In Buber's view we should, where possible, attempt to engage in I–Thou relations, only resorting to the I–It where there is no other alternative.

Although Buber saw himself as a Jewish philosopher, his work has been received as enthusiastically by Christians as it has been by Jews. His legacy is partly *Ich und Du*, his great work of religious existentialism, but it is also the example of his willingness to approach dialogue with an openness that built bridges even with those who opposed him.

Eastern Religions

The term Eastern religion normally refers to those religious traditions that originated in India and China. These include the Dharma faiths of Hinduism, Buddhism, Jainism, and Sikhism as well as Taoism and Confucianism, the two major Chinese religious philosophies. Perhaps the best way to get a sense of them is to look at how they differ from the Abrahamic religions: Judaism, Christianity, and Islam.

Eastern religions are most obviously distinct from the Abrahamic religions in that they are not straightforwardly monotheistic. That is, they are not committed to the idea (sometimes called "exclusive monotheism") that there is a single, indivisible, all-powerful God. The notion of God is, in fact, almost entirely absent from a number of these religions. Confucianism, for example, though it has temples and rituals, makes very little mention of the supernatural, and, in Western terms, is perhaps more akin to a social ethic than a religion. Similarly, the Four Noble Truths of Buddhism — that life is characterized by struggle, that this is caused by our attachment to the world, that suffering can be ended by detachment, and that this can be achieved by following the Noble Eightfold Path — make no reference to God.

The clear counterexample to this non-theism is provided by Hinduism, which, according to one estimate, has 33 million separate gods. However, the situation with Hinduism is complex. In some traditions, it is a monotheistic religion, similar in many respects to the Abrahamic faiths. For example, the devotees of Vaishanavism, perhaps the most popular Hindu denomination, hold that Vishnu is the Supreme Being, the sustainer and restorer of the cosmos. The aim of Vaishnava practice, then, is eternal life in the spiritual realm of "Vaikuntha" — an eternity in service to Vishnu or one of his avatars. Other Hindu denominations, however, have a different view. The followers of Smartism, for example, worship six manifestations of God and believe that all the myriad deities of Hinduism are but aspects of *brahman*, the unchanging, transcendent reality that underpins all existence.

Perhaps the foundational idea that ties these beliefs together — and also Hinduism to the other Dharma faiths — is that worldly life is something to be escaped. Often this is couched in terms of the language of reincarnation, where the purpose of life is to end the cycle of birth and rebirth. For Hindus, this idea is expressed through the notion of *moksha*, the release from desire and unhappiness and an attainment of a union with the Ultimate Reality (or Supreme Being). In Buddhism, it is referenced through the idea of *Nirvana*, an ecstatic state that brings about Enlightenment. And Sikhs aim at establishing a union with God, which means an end to reincarnation.

Eastern religions all manifest clear rules for living. However, in contrast to their Western counterparts, these are not rooted in a divine command. Rather, they are either directed toward the full expression of humanity — as in the case of the Chinese religious philosophies — which will have positive consequences for the social order; or they are a prerequisite for attaining the kind of detachment from the world that enables people to transcend their earthly existence — as is in the case of the Dharma faiths.

Sankara

Sankara, perhaps one of the greatest Indian thinkers, had a profound impact on the history of Hinduism. He espoused a monistic system of thought which held that the "divine ground" of all being is *brahman*, which is indivisible, conscious, eternal, unchanging, and infinite. The self, or *atman*, in its unqualified state as pure consciousness, is identical to brahman, characterized only by being, consciousness, and bliss.

Born: 788 CE, Kaladi, India
Importance: Instrumental in the revival of the Hindu religion
Died: 820 CE, Kedanath, India

What then of the phenomenal world, the world of our everyday life? Sankara held that it is not real in the same sense as brahman, but neither is it pure illusion. Due to our ignorance (*avidya*), we superimpose objects onto *brahman*, creating the apparent diversity of the phenomenal world. We will remain ignorant in this way, and therefore bound by rebirth to our worldly existence, unless we come to knowledge (*vidya*) of the identity of *brahman* and *atman*. As Sankara puts it:

> This bondage can be destroyed neither by weapons, nor by wind, nor by fire, nor by millions of actions — but nothing except the wonderful sword of knowledge that comes from discernment, sharpened by the grace of the Lord.

To a person unfamiliar with Eastern philosophy, all this can seem a little baffling. In particular, if ultimately there is only one indivisible reality, what exactly is the nature of the world of everyday objects? Sankara sheds some light on this question by asking us to consider the traveler who mistakes a rope for a snake. The snake is unreal, illusory, but it is an illusion based on a

Left: The illusion that the rope is in fact a snake is a temporary reality; until we see it as a rope, we treat it as if it were a snake. Until we reach enlightenment, we have to see the everyday world as if it were real.

reality, the existence of a rope. We only come to an awareness of the unreality of the snake once we know about the rope — until then we treat it as a snake. Likewise, until we are liberated by our knowledge of the true nature of *atman* and *brahman*, we are compelled to treat the everyday world as if it were real.

How then does one come to this knowledge? In *Brahmasutrabhasya* (c. 800 CE), Sankara identifies four preconditions for an enquiry into the nature of *brahman*: 1) an ability to distinguish between the eternal and the non-eternal; 2) a renunciation of the enjoyment of the fruits of one's actions; 3) the cultivation of virtues such as self-restraint and peacefulness; and 4) an overriding desire for liberation. He also believed that this quest for knowledge is essentially a religious task. He insisted that it is necessary to study the great Indian sacred writings in order to prepare properly for knowledge that will liberate us. Moreover, a precondition of religious study itself is faith. A commitment to God is a necessary step on the way to knowledge of *brahman*.

Sankara's importance was profound. He was responsible for a revival of the Hindu religion in the face of rising interest in Buddhism and Jainism. Four monasteries that he built remain important centers of Hindu thought and practice, and he retains devotees and followers in both the East and West, including many of India's academic philosophers.

Hinduism

Ramakrishna

In contrast to a philosophical heavyweight such as Sankara, Ramakrishna's reputation as one of the most important figures in the history of Hinduism is based not on the details or sophistication of his religious outlook, but on the fact that it is believed that his teachings were inspired by a life spent in contemplation and communion with God, setting an inspiring example of holiness.

Born: 1836, Hooghly, India
Importance: The inspiration for the Ramakrishna order
Died: 1886, Calcutta, India

It is possible to get a sense of what this contemplation involved by considering what tradition records as his first extended experience of the divine. Shortly after the death of his brother in 1856, Ramakrishna had begun to pray to the Hindu mother-goddess Kali in the hope that she would appear to him in a vision. However, frustrated over a period of time by her non-appearance, he fell into despair, imploring her, "Mother, you've been gracious to many devotees in the past and have revealed yourself to them. Why would you not reveal yourself to me, also? Am I not also your son?" According to tradition, it was only as Ramakrishna contemplated suicide that Kali appeared to him in waves of light, bringing to him peace and an ecstatic experience of divine bliss.

It was out of this experience that Ramakrishna was led to his most important insight. He immersed himself in the practices and rituals of the mystical traditions of many of the other great world religions, and in each case he came into contact with the same absolute God (*Brahman*). He concluded that all religions reveal a different aspect of one single unified God. There is, as it were, a unity in their diversity. The key task for human beings, then, whatever their particular religion, is to come to a realization of God.

This realization is not easily achieved. It requires that people turn away from the temptations of their bodily existence. Sensuous pleasure, greed, cruelty, and other such vices function to bind people to the world of their everyday lives, preventing them from achieving that state of ecstatic devotion that would allow them to contemplate the consciousness of God. Ramakrishna rejected the view that one could improve the world or get close to God by good works. He taught that all that mattered was the spiritual progress of each individual towards God-consciousness.

Ramakrishna's reputation is considerable. However, it is arguable that this is at least as much a consequence of the abilities of his devotees — in particular, Swami Vivekananda — as it is his own talents or achievements. It was Vivekananda who established the Ramakrishna order of monks in 1886, with the blessing of Ramakrishna.

> His whole life was literally an uninterrupted contemplation of God. He reached a depth of God-consciousness that transcends all time and place and has a universal appeal.
>
> Swami Adiswarananda

Regardless, Ramakrishna's life, as an exemplar of ecstatic religion devotion, is arguably unsurpassed in the modern Indian tradition, justifying his reputation as an avatar, or incarnation of a higher being.

Mahatma Gandhi

Mohandas (Mahatma) Gandhi was one of the most admired and influential leaders of the twentieth century. In showing that it was possible to achieve significant political change by passive, nonviolent protest, he inspired a generation of political leaders, including Martin Luther King, Albert Lithuli, and Helder Camara.

Born: 1869, Porbandar, India
Importance: Showed how a philosophy of nonviolence could work politically
Died: 1948, Delhi, India

Gandhi's philosophy of nonviolence (ahimsa) was based partly on his belief that all human beings have souls, no matter how reprehensible their actions. This means that there is always the possibility of appealing to their humanity or fellow-feeling, in order to persuade them to change their views or behavior. Therefore, almost without exception, violence is unnecessary.

Moreover, violence has effects which are either permanent or very hard to reverse. Consequently, for it to be justified, one would need to be absolutely certain of the justice of the position motivating the violence, and also that it would have the desired outcome. However, since human beings are fallible, such a certainty is never available, and therefore violence is ruled out as an appropriate course of action.

Gandhi was fully aware that people are sometimes led to violence by the desperation of the situations that confront them. However, it was Gandhi's view that it isn't possible to separate means from ends in this fashion. If one uses dubious means to attain good ends, inevitably those ends will be compromised and distorted by the immorality that brought them about.

If violence, then, is not the way to solve disputes, or to end great injustices, what will take its place? Gandhi's extraordinary

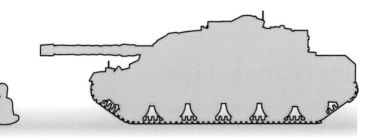

Above: Gandhi's philosophy of "ahimsa" held that almost without exception, violence is unnecessary. Even when confronted by the violence of our oppressors, we should respond nonviolently, in order to open their hearts in the face of suffering.

answer is that one should seek to awaken the essential humanity of an adversary through one's own suffering:

> if you want something really important to be done you must not merely satisfy the reason, you must move the heart also. The appeal of reason is more to the head but the penetration of the heart comes from suffering. It opens up the inner understanding in man. Suffering is the badge of the human race, not the sword.

This idea underpinned his commitment to nonviolent, political protest. Many people will suspect that its utility is limited to very particular circumstances. Nevertheless, if these circumstances obtain, it can be a very powerful mechanism for social and political change, as his own example in India, and that of Martin Luther King in the United States, showed.

On his assassination in 1948, Jawaharlal Nehru, a future prime minister of India, declared "the light has gone out of our lives and there is darkness everywhere."

Hinduism

Guru Nanak Dev

Guru Nanak Dev signaled the formation of the Sikh religion in 1499 with these eight words: "There is no Hindu, there is no Muslim." However, although he is remembered by history as the founder of the youngest of the great world religions, his reputation relies not on this historical contingency but on the wisdom of his appeal to a brotherhood of man.

Born: 1469, Rai Bhoi di Talvandi, Pakistan
Importance: The founder of the Sikh faith
Died: 1539, Kartarpur, India

It would be wrong to suppose that Nanak's Sikhism represented a clean break from either Hinduism or Islam, since it took inspiration from both. In particular, Nanak's belief that salvation is to be understood in terms of an escape from the worldly cycle of birth and rebirth has clear antecedents in Hindu beliefs about reincarnation. Additionally, the central role that meditation plays in his religious thinking has parallels in Hinduism and Sufism.

Nanak's Sikhism, which he preached, according to tradition, while traveling across Asia on four long voyages, is constituted by a number of core practices and beliefs. Perhaps the most significant of these is that its devotees should engage in disciplined meditation with the aim of gaining a divine union with God. Nanak disdained formal ritual, idols, temples, and all the standard external accoutrements of faith. He insisted that meditation should be inward looking and based on the repetition of the divine name of God (*Waheguru*).

The divine name refers to a single, indivisible, omnipresent being. Nanak, in a verse reproduced in the *Guru Granth Sahib*, the holy Scripture of the Sikh faith, described God thus:

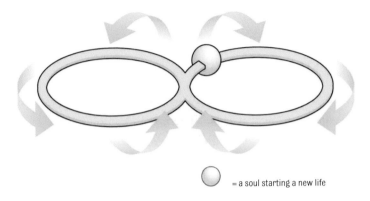

= a soul starting a new life

Above: Sikhs believe in an endless cycle of birth and rebirth, which can be broken through coming into union with God.

He is the supreme truth, He, the Creator, is without fear and without hate. He, the omnipresent, pervades the universe. He is not born, nor does he die again to be reborn. By His grace shalt thou worship Him.

Meditation, then, is the mechanism by which people come into union with God and break the endless cycle of birth and rebirth that is the mark of a worldly existence. In contrast to some other mystical traditions, Nanak did not teach that salvation was dependent on the renunciation of the world. On the contrary, though he thought that purity of the mind had a place in salvation, he emphasized the importance of family, selfless hard work, and charity to contribute to the betterment of humankind.

Nanak's teachings were impressively enlightened in many ways considering that they were established in the fifteenth century. He insisted that all humans were equal in their standing before God, rejecting the significance of caste differences and the authority of a priestly class.

Sikhism

Gobind Singh

Gobund Singh, the last of the living Sikh gurus, transformed the Sikh religion. As well as setting up the Khalsa military order, he also established the Sikh holy book, now considered a "living Guru," as his successor.

Born: 1666, Patnar, Bihar, India
Importance: Created the Khalsa, the military order of Sikhs
Died: 1708, Nanded, Maharashtra, India

Singh had a well-developed sense of the dramatic, which was manifest in the manner in which he established the Khalsa. According to tradition, in front of a great crowd of Sikhs at the Baisakhi festival in Anandpur, he asked whether any one of them would offer up a head to him. Eventually, one man stepped forward, and Gobind Singh disappeared with the volunteer into a tent. He reappeared on his own a few minutes later with his sword covered in blood, asking for a further volunteer. This same process was repeated four more times, after which the Guru reappeared with the five men, all apparently restored to life. Then, as a sign of their selfless dedication to their faith, they were initiated into the Khalsa brotherhood.

Though possibly apocryphal, this story is indicative of the level of commitment that Gobind Singh demanded of the soldier-saints of the Sikh religion. In one of his poems, he described the Khalsa thus:

> He who repeats night and day the name of Him,
> Who has full love and confidence in God,
> Who bestows not a thought on any but one God,
> Whose enduring light is inextinguishable. . .
> He is recognized as a true member of the Khalsa,
> In whose heart the light of the Perfect One shines.

Gobind Singh laid down a formal code of conduct governing membership of the Khalsa. Its injunctions reflect the essential components of the Sikh religion. For example, devotees are enjoined to worship one God and meditate daily on his name. They are also instructed to give ten percent of their income away for religious purposes. More noticeable demands include that hair should not be shaved or cut, and that devotees must at all times be ready to take up arms and to defend the weak.

Gobund Singh was the tenth and last Guru. Believing that faithful Sikhs could find all the spiritual guidance they needed in their holy book, the Guru Granth Sahib, he declared that it, rather than another human, would be his successor. Thus, Sikhism became a religion without a priestly hierarchy, temporal authority was to rest in the hands of the Khalsa. The effects of this decision are still evident today. The Guru Granth Sahib, though watched over by custodians, is available for Sikhs and non-Sikhs alike to read in the gurdwara (the Sikh temple), thereby reaffirming the Sikh commitment to the principle of equality and the universality of their religion.

Guru Gobund Singh's importance in the rise of the Sikh religion can hardly be overstated. By establishing the Khalsa, he instilled military confidence and competence in the Sikhs of the Punjab region and transformed their fortunes. As Khushwant Singh put it in his history of the religion, "Within a few months a new people were born — bearded, beturbanned, fully armed, and with a crusader's zeal to build a new commonwealth."

Khalsa: Khalsa, meaning "pure," was the name used by Guru Gobind Singh for Sikhs baptized or initiated into the Khalsa Brotherhood. They carry at all times the Five Ks (*panj kakke*), which are five items of faith: *Kesh* (hair), *Kanga* (comb), *Kaccha* (undergarment), *Kara* (bangle), and *Kirpan* (sword) and live their lives by the teachings of the Guru.

Sikhism

Gautama Buddha

In the view of Gautama Buddha, the founder of the Buddhist religion, life is characterised by suffering (dukkha). This is the first of Four Noble Truths that he became aware of as he achieved spiritual enlightenment whilst meditating under a fig tree in Buddh Gaya.

Born: Ca. 563 BCE, Kapilavastu, Nepal
Importance: The founder of Buddhism
Died: Ca. 483 BCE, Kusinagara, Nepal

The concept of *dukkha* includes a wide range of things such as physical and mental pain, the frustrations of everyday life, ennui, and unfulfilled desires and expectations.

The Four Noble Truths were set out as if they were the stages in a medical consultation. Thus, if *dukkha* was the diagnosis, the second truth, *samudaya*, has to do with establishing the cause of the disorder. The Buddha argued that the origins of *dukkha* are in our attachment to transient things — material objects, other people, the self, and so on. We experience this attachment as a kind of fundamental ache.

It is just thirst or craving, which gives rise to repeated existence, which is bound up with impassioned appetite, and which seeks fresh pleasure now here and now there . . .

The third Noble Truth tells us of a way to end suffering — through *nirodha*, the cessation of the striving for the transient. This is outlined in the Fourth Truth, described in more detail in the Noble Eightfold Path (which comprises right understanding, right intention, right speech, right action, right livelihood, right effort, right mindfulness, and right concentration).

Perhaps the most general statement of the Buddha's teaching on the best way to live is found in his idea of the Middle Way.

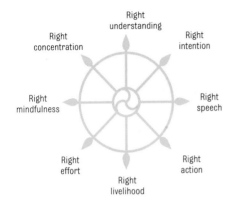

Right understanding

Right concentration

Right intention

Right mindfulness

Right speech

Right effort

Right action

Right livelihood

Left: The Wheel of Dharma is used to demonstrate the Noble Eightfold Path of Buddhism.

Eastern religions commonly state that it is only possible to achieve enlightenment through asceticism and a renunciation of the world. However, after following such a lifestyle for six years, the Buddha came to understand that this was wrong. Instead, he emphasized the fruitfulness of steering a middle path between sensuous indulgence and excessive self-purification.

The practical aspect of the Middle Way can be seen in the type of meditation favored by the Buddha. He did not greatly value the unconscious, trance-like states that were characteristic of many of the traditional meditations. Rather, he espoused *jhuna*, a state of meditation that involves clarity of mind and an experience of bliss.

It is hardly necessary to comment on the influence and historical importance of Gautama Buddha. Buddhism is the dominant religion across Asia. It has also been integral in the development of other religions, in particular Hinduism. Moreover, of the Eastern religions, it is perhaps the most attractive to the Western mindset, since it requires neither that one gives up a commitment to rationality and clear thinking, nor that one renounces the world of everyday life.

Buddhism

Dogen

According to Dogen, perhaps the key figure in the emergence of the Soto branch of Zen Buddhism, the essence of Buddhism lies in its practice. He came to this view after puzzling over what seemed to him to be a paradox connected to the idea of "original awakening." This holds that in some sense we already inhabit our Buddha nature. But if that's the case, then what role is there for Buddhist training and practice?

Born: 1200, Kyoto, Japan

Importance: The founder of the Soto Zen school of Buddhism in Japan

Died: 1253, Kyoto, Japan

Dogen's answer is that practice and enlightenment are identical. It is not necessary to engage in Buddhist practice — which might involve meditation, chanting, or ritual — *in order* to attain enlightenment. Rather, in practice people *are* enlightened; practice and enlightenment are not two different things, but the same thing. In more concrete terms, Dogen emphasized the importance of a particular way of living and of a meditative practice called *zazen*. His injunction to live a particular way was simple:

> When you refrain from unwholesome actions, are not attached to birth and death, and are compassionate to all sentient beings . . . not excluding or desiring anything . . . you will be called a Buddha. Do not seek anything else.

The idea of *zazen*, though, is more complex. In its essence, it is a cross-legged form of meditation that involves a casting off of body and mind. In *zazen* there is no gap between practice and enlightenment. It is not an activity directed towards a particular goal, but rather an end in itself. Dogen explained, "*Zazen* is not thinking of good, not thinking of bad. It is not conscious endeavor . . . Do not desire to become a Buddha."

A significant consequence that flows from the identity of practice and enlightenment is that Dogen's Buddhism requires ongoing effort and commitment. Enlightenment is not something that is to be achieved through one experience; rather it is a way of life that includes the practice of *zazen*. The specific demands that Dogen made of Buddhist monks were stringent. For example, they must give up any desire for material wealth and fame, they should not walk about in the world outside the monastery, they must not speak ill of other people, they must not quarrel, they should always do as requested by their supervisors, they should only wear plain clothing, and they must practice *zazen*.

Soto: The largest Zen sect in Japan. It focuses on Shikantaza as a meditation technique, which requires going beyond the thinking mind to achieve enlightenment.

According to Dogen, there are no barriers of sex, status, or intelligence to prevent people from realizing their Buddha nature. The historical Buddha, Siddhartha, stressed that all living beings are equal in this respect. However, Dogen did think that levels of commitment to the Buddhist way of life make a difference. While he saw no intrinsic barrier to a layperson achieving their Buddha nature, the reality is that they are likely to be too taken up in the activities of everyday life to engage in proper Buddhist practices.

Dogen's influence extends to the present day. Following his death in 1253, Keizan Jokin took up his teachings and brought them to large numbers of people, firmly establishing the Soto sect in Buddhist tradition. In Japan today, the Soto Zen School is one of the two largest existing Buddhist orders.

Vasubandhu

Vasubandhu, one of the greatest of the early Buddhist thinkers, was committed to the somewhat startling view that consciousness is the only reality: that everything that we experience, contemplate, and conceptualize exists only in the mind. This means that people experience the world in different ways, depending upon their emotional makeup, past experiences, associations, and memories.

Born: Ca. fourth century CE, Peshawar, Pakistan.
Importance: One of the founders of the Yogocara Buddhist school of philosophy
Died: Ca. fifth century CE

The obvious objection to this view — which is sometimes called subjective realism — is that it seems that the world determines our experiences, not the other way around. For example, if we visit the same location on more than one occasion, its appearance will tend not to have altered — it will consist of the same objects. Moreover, other people will also tend to see the same objects, and experience the location in a similar way. If there is no external reality, how is this possible?

Vasubandhu's answer in his *Vimshaitika* (Twenty-Verse Treatise, sixth century CE) was that even in dreams we experience the world consistently; and that it is possible for different people to experience the same things even where there are no external objects of thought. His argument to this effect has two stages. First, he argued that hell has a subjective rather than physical reality: its reality cannot be physical, because if it were then the hell-guardians that roam its surface would be in too much pain themselves to torment the damned. Second, he noted that it is nevertheless experienced in the same way by its captives: they all experience the same "river of pus" and "hellish scenes." The only conclusion is that different minds can experience the same things even where these things have only a subjective existence.

Vasubandhu was aware that his consciousness-only teachings might be seen as a departure from the Buddhist view that consciousness emerges in its confrontation with external objects. However, he believed that it was a mistake to think that the Buddha meant this to be taken literally. Not least, it does not make logical sense. Take the notion that reality has an atomic structure — that it is made up of tiny, indivisible elements. Further reflection on this idea shows that it is plagued by inconsistency. For example, if atoms are indivisible, then they cannot have separate sides. But if this is the case, then they cannot join onto one another to form the aggregates that seemingly comprise the objects of the external world.

These arguments are not decisive. Indeed, they were quickly subjected to criticism from within the Buddhist tradition. However, Vasubandhu had another argument to substantiate his consciousness-only view:

> when [people] become awakened by the attainment of a supermundane knowledge free from discriminations. . . . then they truly understand the non-being of those sense objects through meeting with a clear worldly subsequently attained knowledge.

In other words, those people who attain enlightenment have a direct apprehension of the unreality of the world of external objects. In enlightenment, it is understood that dualistic experiences are mental constructions, necessarily illusory. Thus, it was Vasubandhu's view that Buddhist practice aims at removing "contaminations" and "defilements" from the stream of consciousness.

Paganism

The term "pagan" was originally used by Christians in Ancient Rome to describe those people who remained wedded to older polytheistic religious traditions. Its meaning was extended in the Middle Ages to include all non-Abrahamic religious beliefs. Paganism is therefore associated with a departure from religious orthodoxy.

As a result, the term has negative connotations associated with it, which has meant — until recently, at least — that very few people have been willing to accept the designation. However, in the last fifty years or so, Paganism has acquired a more positive meaning, referring to religious and spiritual outlooks that are rooted in a celebration of the divinity of nature.

Perhaps the most interesting early example of this kind of Paganism is Druidism, which flourished in Celtic society some two millennia ago. The Druids were polytheists, who worshipped many aspects of nature, including the sun, the moon, the stars, streams, lakes, the oak, mistletoe, and the tops of hills. Much of what we know about the Druids comes from Julius Caesar's *On the Gallic Wars*. He reported that Druids:

> are concerned with divine worship, the due performance of sacrifices, public and private, and the interpretation of ritual questions . . . The cardinal doctrine which they seek to teach is that souls do not die, but after death pass from one to another.

Archeological evidence suggests that the Druids constructed stone monuments to function as altars and temples in festivals such as those marking the Celtic year.

Druidism proper largely disappeared from Celtic society with the emergence of Christianity in the second century CE. However, interest in Druid beliefs revived in the eighteenth century with the advent of Romanticism, and then again in the twentieth century with the growth of Neo-Paganism.

This latter movement is too diverse to be easily specified. It is fair to say, though, that Neo-Pagans, like the original Druids, typically have a reverential attitude towards nature, and also tend to structure their ritual activities around the changing of the seasons. For example, Wiccan Neo-Pagans celebrate a "fire festival" variant of Imbolc every year at the beginning of February. The term "Imbolc" has various meanings, all of which relate to the notion of renewal. The festival then is a celebration of the approach of Spring, and is marked by the burning of candles and the lighting of home hearth fires.

It is difficult to assess the current level of Pagan belief. There is no single accepted definition of the term, and the institutional structures associated with Paganism are loose. A recent study in the United States found that some 140,000 people self-designated as Pagans; 134,000 as Wiccans; and 33,000 as Druids. This suggests that about 300,000 people self-identify in a way that would make them Neo-Pagan, as this term is commonly understood in the West.

However, this is probably to underestimate the extent of religious belief that is in some sense coterminous with Paganism. Many native religions, for example, share Pagan ideas about the divinity of nature, and much of the spiritual exploration characteristic of the New Age movement is Pagan in character.

Confucius

Whether Confucius is properly considered a religious figure is a matter of some debate. There are Confucian temples where ceremonies and rituals devoted to his memory take place, but he did not claim divinity for himself. Nor did he make much reference to God or the supernatural. Nevertheless, Confucianism, which he inspired, has guided the lives of Chinese people for more than two millennia.

Born: 551 BCE, Ch'ü-fu, Lu, China

Importance: The inspiration for the philosophy named after him, Confucianism

Died: 479 BCE, Lu, China

Confucius lived and worked at a time of social disorder and political upheaval. The ancient feudal system of the Zhou kingdom had disintegrated leaving behind it only warring feudal states. This had led not only to instability in the political system, but also to a sense of moral decay. Confucius's teachings were an attempt to turn this situation around.

Confucius's work is not systematic in the way of much modern religious and social thought, and it is subject to a number of different interpretations. Nevertheless, it is possible to discern some of the key themes. Perhaps the most important has to do with the cultivation of humanity. Confucius believed that social order would flow naturally if the best qualities of humanity were cultivated within the nexus of everyday relationships (particularly as these exist within the context of the family). Here the central ethical concept is *ren*: roughly speaking, the idea that one becomes fully human in the relationships that one has with others when these are characterized by faithfulness (*zhong*) and mutual respect.

> Do not do to others what you do not want done to yourself.
>
> Confucius, *Amulets*

中	Zhong (faithfulness)	孝	Xiao (filial piety)
君子	Junzi (perfect gentleman)	仁	Ren (human-heartedness)
禮	Li (propriety)	理	Yi (righteousness)

Above: Confucius identified several virtues he believed humans should cultivate in order to promote social order and harmony.

Perhaps the most important point here is that virtue cultivated in the private sphere will flow into the public realm. It was Confucius's belief then that the personal is political in the sense that good behavior cultivated in personal relationships will result in political and social stability. Linked to this idea is the notion of "rectification": if rulers rectify their behavior, so as to lead moral lives, they will provide a good example for their subjects. If this is combined with appropriate ritual, a respect for the wisdom of the ancestors, and an appreciation of the power of music and poetry, it will be possible to build a society based on mutual respect and peaceable stability.

The importance of the teachings of Confucius cannot be overstated. They have been, and remain, the wellspring that nourishes Chinese cultural life. The influence of Confucianism extends throughout East Asia, where it is arguably the single most important social, cultural, and religious philosophy, shaping the lives of more than a billion people.

Other Religions

Mahavira Jayanti

Mahavira was the last great Jainist Tirthankar (Enlightened One). He was the final Jainist prophet and is regarded as the man who gave Jainism its present-day form.

Born: Ca. 599 BCE, Kshatriyakundagrama, northeast India
Importance: The reformer and popularizer of Jainism
Died: Ca. 527 BCE, Pavapuri, India

Born into privilege, the son of King Siddhartha and Queen Trishala, Mahavira renounced the materialistic trappings of the world at the age of thirty and began to live a life of extreme asceticism. He had no clothes, no home, and no regular food. He suffered verbal and physical violence and spent a large part of his time fasting and meditating. This lifestyle essentially formed the beliefs that would become systematized as the Jainist religion.

At the core of Mahavira's Jainism is the belief that it is possible to achieve a state of perfect enlightenment (*keval-jnana*) by renouncing all of the desires and behaviors associated with worldly existence. It is only in this way that individuals are able to achieve *nirjara* — the destruction of the "karmic atoms" that bind the soul to its earthly life — the prerequisite of liberation (*moksha*).

Mahavira taught a code of conduct, comprising five vows, to be followed by the devotee seeking liberation. The most interesting is perhaps the injunction to nonviolence (*ahimsa*). It was Mahavira's belief, following the teaching of the twenty-third Tirthankar, Parshva, that to harm another living creature was to interrupt the spiritual progress of their soul (*jiva*). Therefore, it is necessary to take rigorous steps to ensure that this does not occur. For example, a Jainist might refuse to eat after dark, or wear a cloth mouth cover, for fear of accidentally swallowing a living creature. They might walk only with great care in order to avoid stepping on insects. They might take extreme care with their words and deeds in order to avoid causing psychological distress.

The other vows are similarly austere. Jainists are instructed to be always truthful, never to steal, to be chaste — Mahavira added this injunction to the four principles already given by Parshva — and to eschew all attachment to the physical world. This last injunction has far-reaching consequences. It refers not only to material possessions, but also to friends and family. According to tradition, at the start of his spiritual quest, Mahavira abandoned his wife, children, and family, and then later ignored his wife when she attempted to interrupt a period of penance.

There is an interesting general point here about the ethics of Jainism. In one sense, the religion is suffused with the ethical. It demands an ascetic lifestyle, requiring that its devotees live according to a strict moral code. However, as envisaged by Mahavira, Jainism is essentially a personal, spiritual quest, and consequently it is divorced from the concerns of worldly life. There is no injunction to almsgiving, for example, as one finds in Islam and Sikhism. Nevertheless, in the concept of *ahimsa*, which is entirely ethical, one finds perhaps Jainism's most enduring legacy. It was at the heart of Gandhi's philosophy of nonviolence and remains integral to many Buddhist and Hindu traditions. More generally, Jainism lives on as one of the great classical religions of India, counting some four million people — split into two sects, the Shvetambaras and the Digambaras — among its devotees.

Asceticism: Describes a life characterized by self-denial and abstinence from worldly pleasures, often in order to achieve greater spirituality and obtaining a greater connection to the divine.

The Taoist

Lao Tzu

Lao Tzu is a paradoxical figure. It is possible that he did not exist at all. If he did live, then it is possible he didn't write the *Tao Te Ching* (around 600 BCE), one of the most important works in the canon of Eastern religion, despite having been identified as its author for some two millennia. His teachings, as they appear in the *Tao Te Ching* — if indeed they are his teachings — are also full of paradox.

Born: Sixth century BCE
Importance: The original exponent of Taoism
Died: Sixth century BCE

Much of the *Tao Te Ching* is concerned with spelling out correct modes of leadership. Lao Tzu denied that physical force is the best way to achieve political ends. He disavowed an ostentatious ruling style and suggested that a ruler should not attempt to dominate his subjects, but rather should take the mind of the people as his own, harmonize with them, and if necessary conceal his own thoughts. He also argued that a ruler should be as conciliatory as possible: "The gentle and soft overcomes the hard and aggressive."

Lao Tzu's thoughts about leadership are indicative of his general approach. He advocates a quietism that reflects his general conception of the *tao*. The term has two different, though related, meanings: in Confucian thought it refers to the correct path to take for proper human conduct; in Taoism, the concept is broadened so that it denotes the fundamental reality of the Universe, the origin of all things. The precise form taken

> So if you want to be over people
> You must speak humbly to them.
> If you want to lead them
> You must place yourself behind them.
>
> Lao Tzu on leadership

by the *tao*, however, is beyond our capabilities to express in language, or even to conceive. At the beginning of the *Tao Te Ching*, Lao Tzu describes it as follows:

A way that could be named or expressed,
has not the true Essence of the Way.
A name that could be called or sounded,
has not the true Essence of the Name.

The thought arises that if it isn't possible to describe the *tao*, nor even conceive it in thought, perhaps it is an empty concept. However, one of the central tenets of Taoism is that a certain way of living enables one to gain an intuitive understanding of the *tao*. This requires that one live a life of detachment; one must engage in non-action (*wu wei*). It is easy to see how this idea relates to Lao Tzu's thoughts about good leadership. The Universe left to its own devices works harmoniously. Therefore, rulers should always opt for "creative quietude" where this is an option.

The historical Lao Tzu is a shadowy figure. We don't know much about him, and what we do know is mixed up with myth and tradition. However, the Lao Tzu who is believed to have authored the *Tao Te Ching* is to be celebrated as the original exponent of Taoism, one of the three great religions of China, with some twenty million believers worldwide.

Taoism: Exists as both a religion and a philosophical school, though the differences are hard to identify. Tao is central to Taoism: it literally means "path" or "way," but has come to have a more complex and abstract meaning in religion and philosophy.

Zarathustra

Zoroastrianism is not a well-known religion, nor does it have many adherents. It is estimated that there are only 150,000 Zoroastrians remaining in the world, located mainly in India and Iran. However, the religion is notable as the oldest existing example of a monotheistic belief system — a belief system that invokes a single God.

Born: Ca. 628 BCE, Rhages, Iran

Importance: The founder of Zoroastrianism, the oldest existing monotheistic religion

Died: Ca. 551 BCE, Balkh, Afghanistan

Very little is known about Zarathustra, the founder of Zoroastrianism, except that he lived in Bactria — modern day Afghanistan — sometime between 1900 BCE and 600 BCE. His life was transformed when the God Ahura Mazda appeared to him in a vision. As a result of this experience, Zarathustra began to preach the monotheistic view that Ahura Mazda, the uncreated creator of both heaven and earth, was the supreme God and that he alone must be worshipped.

It is in the details of Ahura Mazda's act of creation that many of the specifics of the Zoroastrian religion are found. According to the sacred texts of this faith, at the time of creation, Ahura Mazda created two great spirits who were given the freedom to choose between paths of good and evil. One chose good, the other evil, establishing two great kingdoms, the Kingdom of Justice and Truth, and the Kingdom of the Lie.

For Zarathustra, life was a dualistic struggle between good (or "The Truth") and evil (or "The Lie"). He taught that we are free to choose either the way of Ahura Mazda or of Ahriman (Ahura Mazda's evil counterpart). If we support Ahura Mazda, we will hasten what is believed to be the inevitable victory of good over evil. However, our freedom to choose confers upon us a responsibility for our fate. Zarathustra advised that there would be a Final Judgement, where each one of us will be called to account on how we have lived our lives and either be rewarded or punished in the afterlife (the similarity of this view and the Christian notion of heaven and hell is obvious).

Zarathustra's ideas about the struggle between good and evil have received a modern treatment in Friedrich Nietzsche's famous work *Thus Spake Zarathustra* (1885). However, Nietzsche's portrayal of Zarathustra is notable because it reverses the traditional, morality-based understanding of good and evil.

There is little doubt that Zarathustra's monotheism was influential in the development of subsequent monotheistic religions. His ideas about the fight between good and evil affected the emergence of similar thoughts in the Judeo-Christian tradition. There is also some evidence that Greek thinkers such as Plato and Aristotle were aware of and interested in his doctrines.

> . . . was the first to consider the fight of good and evil the very wheel in the machinery of things: the transposition of morality into the metaphysical realm, as a force, cause, and end in itself, is his work. . . . Zarathustra created this most calamitous error, morality.
>
> Nietzsche, *Ecce Homo*

Animism and Native Religions

Animism is the belief that the things of nature, animate and inanimate alike, have a soul or spirit. In the great monotheistic religions, there is a clear distinction between the sacred and the profane; between that which has a religious nature and that which does not. This is not the case for those cultural and religious traditions based on animism. Animals, plants, the sky, rivers and mountains are all imbued with religious significance.

Animism is the characteristic outlook of many native (indigenous) communities. However, it is not quite right to think that the beliefs and practices of such communities are specifically religious. In a world where there is no gap between the sacred and the profane there is little conceptual space for anything that is distinctively a religion. To the extent that it does make sense to talk of native religions, it is with respect to the beliefs and practices that govern the relationship between living communities and the rest of the natural world.

It is possible to get a sense of what this means by looking at Shinto, the native religion of Japan. Shinto is a polytheistic religion with a vast range of gods or spirits (kami). These include the sun goddess Amaterasu, specific mountains and streams, long dead village elders, and even at one time the reigning emperor. The rituals and practices of Shinto are concerned primarily with honouring the kami, and also averting their anger. This means variously: ritual offerings of food and drink at the Shinto shrine; ceremonial occasions to mark rites of passage; celebrations associated with the passing of the seasons; and elaborate purification rituals, aimed at neutralizing the offence that death, blood, disease, and dirt cause to the kami.

The number of Japanese people who label themselves as Shinto declined in the latter part of the twentieth century. This mirrors a general phenomenon which has seen native religions worldwide coming under pressure from the forces of modernity. This has been particularly acute in the case of Native American religions. The arrival of Europeans in America resulted in the destruction of entire traditions of ritual, ceremony, and narrative. One consequence was the emergence of The Native American church in the late nineteenth century, which combined elements of traditional Native American spirituality with Christian influences, centering them on rituals surrounding the peyote plant.

The Native American church is now the largest indigenous religion in the States. However, the tensions between modernity and tradition remain. In particular, these are manifest in disputes about the ownership of sacred sites and artifacts. It is here that the animism of native religions is significant. It is a Native American belief that sacred sites and artifacts are associated with powerful forces. Therefore, they should be dealt with only under the protection of proper ceremony. Indeed, traditionalists think that real harm has resulted from the removal of artifacts to museums, both to museum staff and visitors, and to the tribes who were properly responsible for the care of these objects.

Animism holds that there is little, if any, difference between the sacred and the profane. Therefore, there are no objects which are not potentially worthy of religious veneration.

Glossary

adherent A believer in a particular idea or religious group.

analogy An attempt to explain something by comparing it to something else.

apostasy The rejection of one's former religion.

commentaries Written explanations of the meaning of something, particularly a written work.

empirical Based on or rooted in observation or experience.

enlightenment A state of true understanding, or the reaching of such a state.

eschatological Having to do with the end of the world and the ultimate fate of humankind.

fallible Capable of being wrong or making mistakes.

fundamentalism Strictly following a set of basic principles, especially those of a particular religion.

internecine Taking place between members of the same country, group, religion, or organization.

jurisprudence The study and theory of law.

meditation Training the mind to reach a calm state for the purposes of relaxation or spiritual growth, often by focusing on a sound, object, thought, or so forth.

monotheism The belief in or worship of a single God.

mysticism The conviction that knowledge of spiritual truth can best be gained by prayer, contemplation, and striving for union with the divine.

omnipotent Having unlimited power or authority.

omniscient Having unlimited knowledge or understanding.

orthodox In accordance with traditional or established customs or beliefs, especially in a religious context.

patriarch A man considered to be an ancestor of the human race or the Hebrew people in the Torah, Bible, or Qur'an.

polytheism The belief in or worship of multiple gods.

precept A rule for how people should behave.

schism A division between people, especially one that divides a religious group based on a disagreement over a particular matter or matters.

sect A subgroup of a larger religious group.

secular Having to with things that are not religious or spiritual in nature.

theology The study of God, or of religion.

For More Information

Canadian Centre for Ecumenism
1819 Bd René Lévesque O
Montréal, QC H3H 2P5
Canada
(514) 937-9176
Website: http://www.oikoumene.ca
This group aims to promote interfaith learning and dialogue. It
has hosted dialogues between clergy of several faiths and
publishes an international quarterly magazine, *Ecumenism*.

Graduate Theological Union
2400 Ridge Road
Berkeley, CA 94709
(510) 649-2400
Website: http://gtu.edu/about
The Graduate Theological Union is a consortium of religious
schools and centers. Its aims include "building bridges among
Christian denominations and other faith traditions, and...
educating students for teaching, research, ministry, and service."

Harvard Theological Review
Harvard Divinity School
45 Francis Avenue
Cambridge, MA 02138
(617) 495-5786
Website: http://hds.harvard.edu/faculty-research/research-
publications/harvard-theological-review
This widely respected journal covers a wide range of topics,
including the Hebrew Bible, New Testament, Christianity,
Jewish studies, theology, ethics, archaeology, and comparative
religious studies.

Hindu American Foundation
910 Seventeenth Street NW, Suite 316A
Washington, DC 20006
(202) 223-8222
Website: http://hafsite.org
The advocacy group represents the more than two million
American Hindus, educating the public about Hinduism and
speaking out about issues that impact Hindus in the United
States and around the world.

Institute of Islamic Studies
Morrice Hall, Room 319
3485 McTavish Street
Montreal, QC H3A 0E1
(514) 398-6077
Website: http://www.mcgill.ca/islamicstudies/
This academic institute was founded in 1952 and is North
America's first institute of Islamic studies. It aims to
"understand the societies and cultures of Islam in an unbiased
way, taking into account the scholarship of Muslims (both
recent and traditional) and that of non-Muslims."

Religion & Ethics Newsweekly
c/o WNET
825 Eighth Avenue
New York, NY 10019
(212) 560-1313
Website: http://www.pbs.org/wnet/religionandethics/
Religion & Ethics Newsweekly is a television show on PBS that
discusses the role of religion and ethics in current affairs. The
program, which first aired in 1997, has won many awards and
aims to cover stories relating to various faiths.

The Rohr Jewish Learning Institute
822 Eastern Parkway
Brooklyn, NY 11213
(718) 221-6900
Website: http://www.myjli.com/index.html
This group's goal is to "make Jewish learning accessible and
personally meaningful to every Jew, regardless of background or
affiliation." It has centers in more than 600 communities and
also offers online classes.

Websites
Because of the changing nature of Internet links, Rosen Publishing
has developed an online list of websites related to the subject of
this book. This site is updated regularly. Please use this link to
access the list:

http://www.rosenlinks.com/THINK/Rel

For Further Reading

Edelglass, William, and Jay Garfield, eds. *Buddhist Philosophy: Essential Readings*. New York, NY: Oxford University Press, 2009.

González, Justo L. *A History of Christian Thought*. Nashville, TN: Abingdon Press, 2014.

Green, Nile. *Sufism: A Global History*. Hoboken, NJ: Wiley-Blackwell, 2012.

Griffith, R. Marie. *American Religions: A Documentary History*. New York, NY: Oxford University Press, 2007.

Jackson, Roy. *What Is Islamic Philosophy?* New York, NY: Routledge, 2014.

Mandair, Arvind-Pal Singh. *Sikhism: A Guide for the Perplexed*. New York, NY: Bloomsbury Academic, 2013.

Manekin, Charles, and Robert Eisen. *Philosophers and the Jewish Bible*. (Studies and Texts in Jewish History and Culture). Potomac, MD: University Press of Maryland, 2008.

Pojman, Louis P., and Michael Rea. *Philosophy of Religion: An Anthology*. 7th Edition. Stamford, CT: Cengage Learning, 2014.

Rose, Jenny. *Zoroastrianism: An Introduction*. (Introductions to Religion). New York, NY: I. B. Tauris, 2011.

Sarma, Deepak. *Classical Indian Philosophy: A Reader*. New York, NY: Columbia University Press, 2011.

Van Norden, Bryan W. *Introduction to Classical Chinese Philosophy*. Cambridge, MA: Hackett Publishing Co., 2011.

Yamakage, Motohisa. *The Essence of Shinto*. 2nd Edition. New York, NY: Kodansha USA, 2012.

Index

For main entries see contents page. References to religious thinkers and leaders are given only where mentioned other than their main entry.